Geography

GCSE

A GUIDE FOR TEACHERS

THE OPEN UNIVERSITY PRESS

SEC Steering Committee

William Kirk (Chairman)
Rod Archer
Trevor Bennetts (HMI)
Diarmid Campbell
Peter Davies
Mary Grant
Peter Jackson
Lesley Tumman
Philip White
John Yockney
Patricia Wilson (Principal Professional Officer)
Jennifer Hill (Secretary)

SEC Team

Sir Wilfred Cockcroft (Chairman and Chief Executive)
Paul Armitage
Gerry Callen
Peter Dines
Ann Harris
John Johnson
Lesley Mach
Denise Williams

Writers

Keith Orrell
Harry Tolley

OU Team

Desmond Nuttall (Director)
Sally Baker
Joan Carty
Diana Harden
Peter Heatherington
Tim Horton
Richard Hoyle
Mike Levers
Kate Laughton
Ken Little (BBC)
Roger Lowry
Ken Patton (BBC)
Bill Prescott
Peter Scrimshaw
Sue Sheldon
Tony Walton
Geoff Wheeler (BBC)

Acknowledgements

Grateful acknowledgement is made to the following for material used in this guide.

Page 11: Table 2 courtesy of Midland Examining Group. *Page 12:* Figure 1a courtesy of East Anglian and London Regional Examining Group. *Page 13:* Figure 1b courtesy of Midland Examining Group. *Page 15:* Figure 2 courtesy of Northern Examining Association. *Page 18:* questions from University of Cambridge Local Examinations Syndicate; cartoon (left) Norman Thelwell and Methuen Ltd; cartoons (right) Punch Publications. *Page 23:* Table 3 courtesy of Scottish Examination Board. *Page 25:* photograph © K. Orrell. *Page 30:* Figures 5a and 5b and questions courtesy of East Anglian Examinations Board/University of Cambridge Local Examinations Syndicate. *Page 31:* Figure 6 and questions courtesy of East Midland Regional Examinations Board/University of Cambridge Local Examinations Syndicate. *Page 35:* Kesteven and Grantham Girls' School and Walton Girls' County Secondary School for the coursework assignment on natural hazards. *Pages 35–37:* Geography Department, Rushcliffe Comprehensive School, Nottingham, for the litter survey material. *Page 40:* Geography Department, Harry Carlton Comprehensive School, East Leake, Nottingham, for information on the use of computers in the coursework assignment on employment. *Page 43:* Figure 10 courtesy of the Geography Department, Northampton Girls' School. *Pages 45–47:* Geography Department, Ecclesbourne School, Duffield, Derby, for information on computerized record keeping and for Figures 11 and 12.

The Open University Press, Walton Hall, Milton Keynes MK7 6AA
First published 1986
Copyright © 1986 Secondary Examinations Council
Printed in Great Britain by Thomson Litho Ltd, East Kilbride, Scotland.
ISBN 0 335 15478 6

1.1

Contents

Introduction

This guide has been prepared by the Open University on behalf of the Secondary Examinations Council. It is intended for the use of all teachers of geography preparing students for the new GCSE examinations, which are to be first held in summer 1988. It describes briefly the novel features of the GCSE system of examining, especially the national criteria that are to be used within that system. Through activities, it prompts the analysis and discussion of current approaches to examinations in geography and of the new approaches that may be employed in the GCSE. In particular, it looks at those issues in geography that are likely to feature most highly in your mind as you prepare to teach courses leading to GCSE examinations.

The guide is designed principally for use in preparation for and during locally organized in-service training courses and seminars. It is organized into four sessions, each designed to form the basis of about half a day's work at such courses or seminars. But the guide can also support individual study or other patterns of group learning, since the activities are generally suitable for individual or group work. However, as the guide will be used by people of very varied experience, from students in their final year of training to experienced heads of department, not all the activities will be appropriate to every reader and so you should do only those that interest or challenge you.

The guide is intended to stimulate thought and discussion, not to provide instant answers to problems and challenges. Nor is it designed to prepare you to assess *particular* GCSE syllabuses—that is the responsibility of the Examining Groups; it is concerned with issues of principle, not with the details of individual syllabuses and their implications.

One aspect of the new GCSE system is omitted from this guide, namely the move towards a system of grade criteria. Put briefly (and hence rather simply) this requires the standards expected of candidates to be specified in detail in advance of the assessment, to help examiners and assessors and to let all users of the examinations know what is required of candidates achieving certain grades. Although work on the development of detailed grade criteria has already begun, it is likely to be some years before a system of grade criteria can be introduced in geography. As a result, grade criteria cannot be discussed in this guide.

While studying this guide you will find it helpful to have available a copy of the National Criteria for geography and copies of current GCE O-level and CSE syllabuses and question papers. You will also find it helpful to view the two videos, one on differentiation and the other on coursework, that accompany this guide. If you can view them, it is best to do so near the beginning of your study of Sessions 2 and 3 respectively. An authoritative statement of the major characteristics of the new GCSE system of examining can be found in *General Certificate of Secondary Education: a general introduction* (Department of Education and Science/Welsh Office, 1985), which has been distributed widely to schools and colleges.

Geography in the GCSE

1.1 The national criteria

A major innovation of the new system is the introduction of national criteria governing all GCSE syllabuses. These criteria are in two parts. First, there are the General Criteria, which set out the framework for all Mode 1, 2 and 3 syllabuses and examinations, as well as a number of ground rules for the conduct of examinations, such as eligibility for entry, a mechanism for appeals, and provision for handicapped candidates. Second, there are criteria specific to each of twenty subjects, including geography, which lay down requirements for every GCSE syllabus in those subjects. These requirements cover five areas: the aims of courses leading to the GCSE, assessment objectives, content, the relationship between assessment objectives and content, and techniques of assessment.

The subject-specific criteria are not written at the level of detail of an examination syllabus, let alone a teaching syllabus, and therefore still leave much freedom to syllabus developers, particularly in the choice of content and techniques of assessment.

Whereas, in the past, the choice of content has tended to dominate the process of syllabus development, the emphasis has now changed with the result that considerable effort has been spent on articulating the aims and assessment objectives of courses and on working out the implications of these aims and objectives for techniques of assessment. Those developing the national criteria have tried to ensure that the assessment objectives can *all* be satisfactorily assessed and that the range of assessment techniques used will not narrow or distort teaching and learning. The cardinal principle governing the choice of assessment techniques is 'fitness for purpose'. As the General Criteria (para. 19(e)) prescribe, 'the principle of fitness for purpose must be observed: all examination components and assessment procedures should reflect and be appropriate to the nature of the subject, its educational aims and its assessment objectives'.

The application of this principle means that, as virtually every subject includes at least one objective that is not easily tested in timed written examinations, the national criteria in almost all subjects, including geography, provide for GCSE examinations to include a significant element of coursework, assessed by the teacher and moderated by an Examining Group.

1.2 The General Criteria and curriculum innovation

As you will be aware from the extensive consultation exercises, the national criteria represent a consensus between the teaching profession, the Examining Groups and Boards, the users of examination results, the Secondary Examinations Council and the Government. The criteria are framed in such a way as to allow considerable freedom to Examining Groups and teachers to develop different syllabuses and schemes of assessment. They are also framed to ensure that the criteria themselves can develop and that curriculum innovation is not stifled. The General Criteria (para. 6) contain the provision outlined overleaf.

The Secondary Examinations Council, acting in consultation with the Examining Groups, is responsible for keeping the National Criteria under review and for advising the Secretary of State for Education and Science and the Secretary of State for Wales on extensions to and changes in the criteria, including grade criteria for individual subjects. The Council will also be able to make recommendations to the Secretaries of State for temporary dispensations from individual provisions of the National Criteria where the Council is satisfied that this is necessary in order that promising innovations in syllabuses or assessment procedures may be tested.

The General Criteria also make provision for GCSE examinations linked to national curriculum projects, and for Mode 2 and Mode 3 examinations.

The General Criteria stipulate the requirements on aims, appropriate width of content and skills, and the format and presentation of a syllabus. They also make it clear that the Examining Groups, acting in consultation with the Secondary Examinations Council, are expected to avoid the unnecessary proliferation of both subject titles and syllabuses.

One of the main purposes of the national criteria is, then, to create a greater commonality in aims, objectives, content and assessment methods for the benefit of candidates, teachers and users alike, while still allowing for development and experimentation. At the same time, the national criteria can be a potent method of spreading good practice and meeting current concerns. For example, the General Criteria (para. 19) include the following requirements:

Avoidance of bias
Every possible effort must be made to ensure that syllabuses and examinations are free of political, ethnic, gender and other forms of bias.

Recognition of cultural diversity
In devising syllabuses and setting question papers Examining Groups should bear in mind the linguistic and cultural diversity of society. The value to all candidates of incorporating material which reflects this diversity should be recognised.

For guidance on this you could consult the University of London School Examination Board's publication *Sexism, Discrimination and Gender Biases in GCE Examinations* (1985) and the Geographical Association's report on *Geographical Education for a Multicultural Society* (Walford, 1985).

ACTIVITY 1

1 What evidence are you aware of which would indicate that there is gender bias in the teaching of geography? As a starting point for discussion you might consider each of the following:
    (a) textbooks and other resources;
    (b) existing geography examinations;
    (c) classroom interaction;
    (d) subject content of syllabuses;
    (e) the process of subject choice at 14 +.

2 How could gender bias be eliminated from geography courses at this and other levels?

3 The central theme of the Swann Report (Department of Education and Science, 1985) is 'education for all', that is a multicultural

education for a multicultural community. What contribution does geography already make to that end? How might its contribution be increased by means of the new examination?

1.3 The National Criteria for geography

For some twenty years geography teachers have been living with changes in the nature of the subject, how it is assessed and consequently how it is taught. In the late 1960s model-based approaches and quantitative techniques were introduced. More recently there has been a renewed interest in area studies at different scales, and new approaches are drawing upon humanistic, behavioural, welfare and radical geography. These developments have brought sweeping changes in A-level GCE courses and examinations, which inevitably are sensitive to changes in the subject in higher education. For the teacher of students aged fourteen to sixteen, change has come through the gradual development of existing examinations, the availability of new teaching/learning resources and especially through the growing acceptance of the philosophies, approaches and examinations of Schools Council projects.

It is unlikely, then, that you will find much that is totally unfamiliar to you in the National Criteria for geography, even if the O-level and CSE courses you run at present do not conform closely to them. Indeed, it would be reasonable to characterize the National Criteria as a synthesis of the major changes in the geography curriculum, including its assessment, which have taken place over the last two decades. Through a single national examinations system, they will make these changes more widely available to all students.

1.4 The rationale for geography in the GCSE

The National Criteria for geography will have most impact upon your work in planning and managing classroom activities. At this stage, then, it would be useful if you could familiarize yourself with these Criteria.

It is tempting when looking at any statement concerned with examinations to turn quickly to those sections to do with content and assessment objectives. However the first two sections of the National Criteria ('Introduction' and 'Aims') perhaps give a better indication of the kinds of school geography it is hoped to encourage. The next activity is designed to help you compare the rationale behind the National Criteria for geography with your own views on the geography curriculum and with the examination schemes you currently follow.

ACTIVITY 2

Read through Sections 1 and 2 ('Introduction' and 'Aims') of the National Criteria for geography. These sections seek to establish an acceptable definition of the subject, the contribution it can make to students' education and the aims which should form the basis of teaching/learning programmes. Make a list of, or underline, all the key phrases which appear novel and problematic when considered against the aims of your existing examination syllabuses. Make a similar list of, or put brackets round, all those phrases which are familiar or non-problematic. For instance, you might feel that the opening sentence of paragraph 1.2, which states that 'Geographical education may be seen in terms of knowledge and understanding, skills and values', proposes three familiar elements of the subject, but that a fourth, 'values', is not usually explicitly referred to in syllabus statements.

If you are working in a group, you could compare your analysis with that of your colleagues.

If you undertake Activity 2 in a large group, there is likely to be a variety of responses, depending on the examination you currently use and your personal views about the geography curriculum. We see the following areas as presenting some novel issues for the management and teaching of the curriculum:

1 The emphasis given to the influence on geographical situations of the values and attitudes of those involved.

2 The relevance of geography to students being educated in a society faced by major issues such as those associated with population change, contrasts in development, resource use and environmental quality.

3 The contribution of geography to education in a multicultural society.

4 The role of geography in the development of skills.

5 Compulsory fieldwork and practical work.

Like us, you are probably pleased to note that all courses *must* include physical as well as human elements and that an understanding of *real* places is an essential goal for geographical education. You may also feel that in the past syllabus statements have not always included such a comprehensive exposition of their rationale and aims.

1.5 Aims and assessment objectives

In any well-ordered statement concerned with the curriculum or examinations the rationale, aims and objectives should be clearly interrelated. It is not essential or indeed desirable that all the aims should be directly matched by assessment objectives. Aims should give direction and purpose to the teaching programme, while assessment objectives have a narrower significance. One way of familiarizing yourself with the aims and objectives in the National Criteria for geography is suggested in Activity 3.

ACTIVITY 3

Select key statements in the 'Introduction' (Section 1) and attempt to identify if and how these statements are translated into 'Aims' (Section 2) and 'Assessment objectives' (Section 3). This activity could be developed by matching statements in the introduction with appropriate aims and assessment objectives by completing a table like the one which has been started opposite.

Table 1

Introduction	Aims	Assessment objectives
'The character of places, the complex nature of people's relationships and interactions with their environment' (para. 1.1).	'To develop a sense of place and an understanding of relative location' (para. 2.1.1)	'An examination shall test the extent to which candidates are able to ... recall specific facts relating to the syllabus content and demonstrate locational knowledge' (para. 3.1).

and so on

If you are doing this activity with colleagues, discuss your responses.

Your responses to Activities 2 and 3 will depend very much on whether your existing syllabuses are long-standing, recently revised to conform to the early draft National Criteria or based on the work of the Geography 14–18 (Bristol) Project or the Geography for the Young School Leaver (GYSL) (Avery Hill) Schools Council Project. Whatever your response, you will probably agree that in the past some syllabus statements have not included such a full exposition of their rationale, aims and objectives as it seems they will be required to do when the National Criteria are operational. It should be remembered that in future all syllabuses will have to conform to the National Criteria. This should lead to a greater similarity of aims and assessment objectives and also encourage Examining Groups to present a more comprehensive statement of them.

For the next activity you will need a selection of geography CSE, O-level or joint GCE/CSE syllabuses.

ACTIVITY 4

Read the sample syllabus statement on aims and objectives given below and look at any other syllabuses you have available.

1 Are they fundamentally different from each other in the approach to geography they represent or do they differ only in fullness, emphasis and detail?

2 Do they differ in a crucial way from paragraphs 1, 2 and 3 of the National Criteria?

3 Do they support the view put earlier that the National Criteria are a synthesis of the major changes in the geography curriculum which have taken place over the last two decades?

Sample syllabus statement
Aims
The aim of the course is to promote [through a conceptual approach] an understanding of the world in which we live by fostering personal awareness of the interrelationship between the environment and man.

Assessment objectives
Candidates will be required to demonstrate their ability to:
(a) recall a body of knowledge.
(b) present information by the use of annotated sketch maps, diagrams, graphs, statistics and in the written form.
(c) recognize, understand and analyse information from direct observation and from the following source materials: maps (including Ordnance Survey maps), photographs, diagrams, statistics, graphs and written material.
(d) use and interpret information by selection, classification, generalization (making and testing hypotheses) and evaluation.

(South Western Examinations Board 1986 CSE Mode 1 Geography Schemes of Examination, Geography A—1110, pp. 2–3)

1.6 The guidelines on content

In the 'Introduction' to the National Criteria for geography (para. 1.6) it is made clear that there are a number of acceptable approaches in the subject. In the guidelines on content, this flexibility of approach is reiterated: 'satisfactory syllabuses can be structured in terms of systematic themes illustrated regionally, as well as of regions within which selected topics are studied' (para. 4.1). Other basic content structures should also be acceptable in the light of this enabling statement. Whatever proposals for syllabus content emerge, they will have to follow the guidelines set out in paragraph 4.1. These seem to indicate that the following are essential:

1 Fieldwork in a small area (para. 4.1.1).

2 Selected contrasting area and thematic studies within the British Isles (para. 4.1.2).

3 Studies of the United Kingdom's links with wider groupings of nations (para. 4.1.3).

4 Studies of relevant contemporary issues (para. 4.1.4).

5 Studies which focus on the interaction between people and their environments (para. 4.1.5).

The content criteria at first sight are not heavily prescriptive, but you should remember that the Examining Groups, in translating the criteria into operational syllabuses, will wish to spell out the content much more fully.

In what ways might the content be specified? Some current syllabuses give very clear guidance on content by comprehensively listing the regions or topics to be studied. At the other extreme, some syllabuses provide only guidelines for selection of syllabus content and encourage schools to plan their own detailed teaching syllabuses. Those following the Geography 14–18 (Bristol) Project's O-level and Joint GCE/CSE Examination are provided with a minimum of direction and are encouraged to use Table 2 to plan their own teaching programmes based on the aims of the core syllabus.

Notice that this table gives guidance on appropriate 'systematic' content areas (column A), the relevant systems and processes to be considered (column B) and the selection and weighting of areas and scales to be studied (column C). In its O-level syllabus document the GYSL (Avery Hill) Project uses a framework of key ideas. These are broad generalizations which are useful in the interpretation of a variety of geographical situations. For example, one such key idea related to patterns of urban growth is that 'there are certain characteristics of cities that appear to be universal: (i) outward sprawl; (ii) competition for land at the centre resulting in high rise development; (iii) the problem of adequate provision for housing and transport due to rapid growth'. The syllabus suggests suitable content for the exploration of key ideas but encourages teachers to select their own, at three scales: local, regional, and global.

Several of the joint GCE O-level/CSE syllabuses which are being developed by the new Examining Groups and which are likely to form the basis of their proposals for GCSE seem to develop the GYSL approach. The next activity asks you to consider alternative approaches to setting out syllabus content.

Table 2 Structure of the core syllabus for the Geography 14–18 (Bristol) Project's examinations.

A	B	C
Illustrative examples to be chosen from	Wider systems or contexts to be considered	Appropriate distribution of examples chosen
(i) Weather and climate	Atmospheric and oceanic circulation	Local and British Isles 40 per cent–50 per cent approximately
(ii) Contrasting landforms	Longer-term geologic and short-term geomorphic processes	Other developed regions of the world 15 per cent–30 per cent approximately
(iii) Conservation of natural resources	Hydrologic cycle	
(iv) Agricultural land-use		
(v) Location, growth and decline of industries	Physical	
(vi) Transport networks	Techno-logical processes influencing	
(vii) Economic growth and trade	Economic spatial patterns and	Less developed regions of the world 15 per cent–30 per cent approximately
(viii) Settlement patterns between and within towns	Social landscapes Political	
(ix) Population growth and distribution		Wider physical and economic systems at a world scale 10 per cent–15 per cent approximately

Source: Midland Examining Group 1987 Syllabus for Joint GCE O-level/CSE Examination, Geography (Bristol Project), Table 1, p. 8.

ACTIVITY 5

Figures 1a and 1b are extracts from syllabuses currently being developed for GCSE. Both consciously avoid giving prescriptive lists of areas and topics. They do, however, emphasize issues and key ideas to be studied and the need to study these at a variety of scales. The extracts represent the main element of physical geography in their respective syllabuses, although the role of the environment is recognized in other units.

Figure 1a is from the East Anglian and London Regional Examining Group's Joint GCE O-level/CSE for 1987, Syllabus A. The syllabus has three compulsory modules and a fourth one to be chosen from five options. The syllabus states that 'the selection of locations for specific studies may be made according to the teacher's specialisms and interests and the available resources'. An example of appropriate locations for some of the modules is included in the syllabus document to assist teachers to plan their courses.

Figure 1a Extract from East Anglian and London Regional Examining Group's 1987 Joint GCE O-level/CSE Syllabus A for Geography, p. 5.

COMPULSORY CORE MODULE — LANDSCAPES AND WATER

Heading	Key Ideas	Commentary
Systems	1. The world's water supply is contained within a closed system — the water cycle.	The components of the water cycle include precipitation, run-off and evapo-transpiration.
	2. Individual drainage basins form dynamic open systems with inputs, throughputs and outputs.	The system structure of drainage basins permits the analysis of water movement in terms of stores, flows and losses.
Classification	3. Landforms and landscapes associated with rivers and river valleys and coastal zones may be classified according to their characteristic appearances and to the processes which form them.	Processes include weathering, mass movement, erosion, transport and deposition. The landforms created may also be influenced by rock type and structure.
Spatial Patterns	4. The natural availability of water varies from place to place.	Physical factors include rainfall patterns and river systems.
	5. There is often a mis-match between supply and demand.	Areas of high water supply often occur in remote, thinly populated and/or mountainous regions.
Dynamics	6. The supply and distribution of water can change as a result of natural fluctuations and human intervention in the water cycle.	Changes may include floods, their causes, effects and control; drought and the process of desertification; water management schemes; pollution.
	7. Competing demands for water can create conflicts, both environmental and economic.	These may be local (e.g. flooding a valley for a reservoir), national (e.g. water transfer schemes) or international (e.g. drainage basin boundary conflicts)
	8. Natural and man-made changes to the coastal zone may create opportunities and/or problems.	Opportunities include resort development; new port sites; land reclamation. Problems include cliff recession; silting of ports; the need for sea defences; pressures of tourism.

Figure 1b is from the Midland Examining Group's Joint GCE O-level/CSE Syllabus for 1987. This is the content statement for one of three sections. Part of the syllabus rationale is linked to the content. Examples of areas and topics considered suitable for the teaching of each section of the syllabus are provided.

Figure 1b   Extract from Midland Examining Group's 1987
Joint GCE O-level/CSE Syllabus for Geography, pp. 5–6.

SECTION A : PEOPLE AND THE PHYSICAL ENVIRONMENT

GENERAL RATIONALE

It is important that candidates appreciate and understand landscapes and ecosystems, and the way people interact with them, in order that they may develop a sensitive awareness of physical environments. Through a study of these environmental systems and the human pressures on them it is intended that candidates become aware of the vulnerability of physical environments.

In studying this section of the syllabus candidates should develop an appreciation of the issues and an understanding of the key ideas listed below.

ISSUES

1. The distinctive characteristics and qualities of landscapes and the need for their conservation.

2. Increasing human pressure from rapid population growth, changing population distribution, technological change and increasing leisure time, is changing natural landscapes and ecosystems.

3. Management of landscapes and ecosystems is required for their optimum use.

4. The causes of natural hazards: their prediction and amelioration of their effects.

5. The inter-action of human activities and environments and the opportunities and constraints different people face in their different environments.

KEY IDEAS

A. Plates. The earth's crust is made up of a number of plates whose margins are marked by tectonic, seismic and volcanic activity and their associated landforms.

B. Slopes. Slopes vary in form and scale and change through time as a result of a variety of weathering and various mass movement processes.

C. Basins. Fluvial processes operate in the drainage basin within the wider hydrological cycle.

D. Atmosphere. Weather and climate have important effects upon physical processes and human activities.

E. Environments. Distinctive environments develop from the inter-action of earth, atmosphere, plants and animals. People affect these inter-actions and change natural environments.

CONTENT

A study of the following content is considered appropriate for candidates to gain an appreciation and understanding of the issues and key ideas at small, medium and large scales.

(a) **Plates**   The global pattern of plates, their structure, boundaries and motions. The processes associated with seismic, volcanic and tectonic activity and their effects on landscapes.

(b) **Slopes**   The development of slopes in areas of different rocks and in contrasting environments including humid temperate, glacial and coastal.

(c) **Basins**   The hydrological cycle and the drainage basin as a system (inputs, outputs and movements through). Channel and valley processes and landforms.

(d) **Atmosphere**   Meteorological processes and their effects on people and the physical environment in the British Isles.

(e) **Environments**   The components, productivity and inter-action within ecosystems. The study of characteristics and processes in contrasting ecosystems.

The study of content should be illustrated by examples which relate to one or more of the following scales as indicated below.

Content	Small Scale (within a small area)	Medium Scale (regional/national)	Large Scale (continental/global)
Plates	✓	✓	✓
Slopes	✓	—	—
Basins	✓	✓	—
Atmosphere	✓	✓	—
Environments	✓	✓	✓

CONTENT EXEMPLARS

Some possible content exemplars, illustrating the issues, key ideas and content from this section of the syllabus in a teaching programme will be published with the specimen questions. These Guidelines relate to the published National Criteria for Geography.

Clearly these two examples are different in their approaches to detailing syllabus content. Look carefully through the two extracts and then consider the following questions:

1 How do these statements seek to meet the requirements of the National Criteria?

2 In what ways are they similar or different?

3 Do they form a sound basis for planning the physical elements of a teaching programme?

As the Examining Groups seem to be pursuing a policy of encouraging teachers to choose their own area/case studies, it would be a useful simulation exercise to prepare for GCSE by trying to plan in outline part of a course based on a statement on physical geography from a proposed GCSE syllabus. You should be sure to refer to the elements of content listed in paragraphs 4.1.1 to 4.1.5 of the National Criteria for geography.

1.7 Techniques of assessment

The key issues raised in this section of the National Criteria (para. 6) are:

1 All Mode 1 schemes of assessment must include a school-based component which accounts for at least 20 per cent of the marks and is designed to assess achievements not easily measured by board-based components. Fieldwork must be part of this school-based component (paras 6.1, 6.2.1, 6.3.1, 6.3.2).

2 Data response/stimulus questions are seen as appropriate means of assessing achievements in a geography which emphasizes the ability to apply skills and ideas to an interpretation of geographical situations (para. 6.2.2).

3 Schemes of assessment must be designed not only to discriminate between candidates but also to measure their positive achievements—what they *can* do rather than what they cannot do—which requires the provision of differentiated assessment tasks (para. 6.4). The question of differentiation is taken up in another part of this guide.

It is interesting to note that the National Criteria specify only the minimum percentage of marks to be allocated to school-based assessment so that it would be possible for GCSE schemes to allocate a higher percentage of marks to coursework. This would of course have drawbacks as well as advantages, and these issues are discussed in a later session.

1.8 The role of fieldwork in GCSE geography

Although geography teachers are quite accustomed to conducting fieldwork, it has not been universally adopted into schemes of examination because of its associated management and resource problems. However, those examinations which do incorporate a fieldwork component almost invariably require an approach that stresses the use of enquiry skills. For instance, the Northern Examining Association's Joint GCE/CSE Examination includes an internally assessed fieldwork component accounting for 25 per cent of the marks. Candidates are encouraged to base their studies on the approach in Figure 2, which provides guidance to teachers on the general conduct of the fieldwork component.

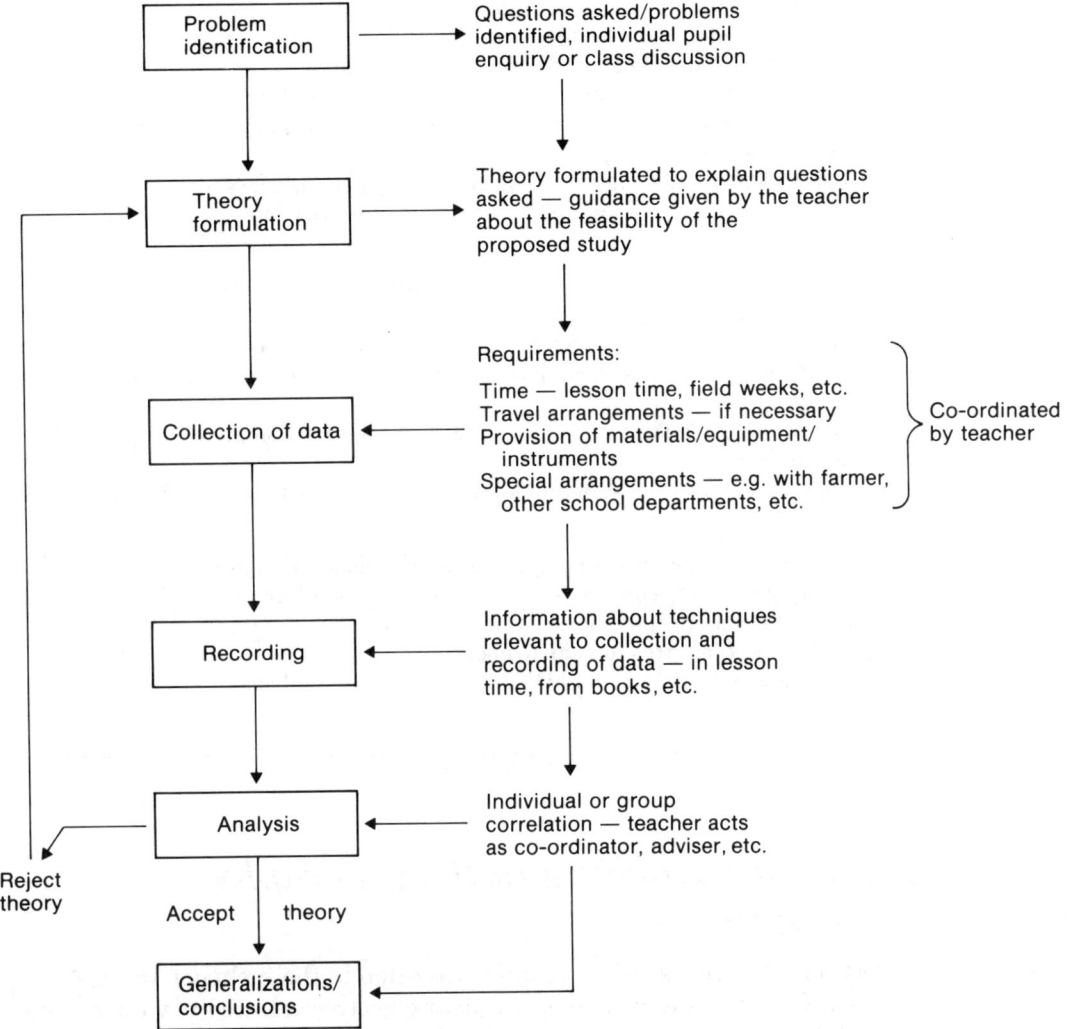

Figure 2   Diagram to illustrate the general approach required from a candidate submitting a personal fieldwork record for the Northern Examining Association's Joint GCE/CSE Examinations.

While fieldwork lends itself very well to the achievement of several of the skills objectives, it would be against the spirit of the National Criteria if fieldwork came to be seen only as a device for assessing a limited range of assessment objectives. Paragraph 1.5 of the National Criteria states that fieldwork 'should always be an integral part of the course'.

ACTIVITY 6

Overleaf is a list of some objectives for fieldwork. Look through the list and then try to match the objectives of any fieldwork you currently undertake with the objectives listed. Does your fieldwork programme cover all or only a few of the objectives in the list? Do you cover some of them incidentally rather than by intention? What teaching/learning strategies could you use to develop a more positive approach to those objectives you currently neglect?

Attitudinal and aesthetic objectives
To arouse students' curiosity.
To develop favourable attitudes towards learning.
To provoke students to ask questions and identify problems.
To sharpen students' perception and appreciation of changing geographical landscapes.
To give students the experience of the pleasure of discovery.
To enjoy the study of geography and acquire a deeper interest in the subject.

Knowledge objectives
To develop better understandings of the nature of things discussed in the classroom and in books.
To enable students to observe and think, and acquire knowledge.
To understand the relationships between physical features and human activities.
To associate the different phenomena which together comprise the geography of an area.
To develop an awareness of problems relating to human occupance of the land.

Skill objectives
To develop an understanding of geographical modes of inquiry.
To distinguish between necessary and extraneous information.
To orient a map in the field.
To relate real features to map symbols.
To develop skills in data collection, recording and analysis.

(Laws, 1984, p. 136)

1.9 Values teaching in the geography curriculum

In Section 1.4 of this session we drew attention to the inclusion in the National Criteria of aims and assessment objectives related to values (paras 2.3 and 3.7). The question of values teaching in the geography curriculum is potentially more significant to the future of our students than was the debate over quantitative techniques and model-based approaches, and the National Criteria have brought this issue to the attention of all concerned with teaching and assessment.

In the next part of this session you will be considering various teaching strategies employed in values education, some of the arguments for a more positive approach to values education and the questions to be borne in mind when planning learning activities.

ACTIVITY 7

Brian Maye summarizes below the variety of approaches to values education used in schools.

Values inculcation has the objective that students will adopt a predetermined set of values.

Values analysis uses structured discussion and logical analysis of evidence to investigate values issues.

Moral reasoning provides opportunities to discuss reasons for value positions and choices with the aim of encouraging growth in moral reasoning ability.

Values clarification has the objective of helping students become aware of their own values in relation to their behaviour and that of others.

Action learning encourages students to see themselves as interacting members of social and environmental systems through having them analyse and clarify values with the intention of enabling them to act in relation to social and environmental issues according to their value choices.

(Maye, 1984, p. 34)

Which of these approaches are implied by the National Criteria for geography, especially paragraphs 2.3 and 3.7?

Try to identify classroom activities which you use or are familiar with which intentionally—or unintentionally—adopt any of the five approaches.

What problems are associated with these approaches?

Is it possible to assess the outcomes of all of these approaches?

In the past some teachers have avoided considering the role of values in geography in an attempt to appear neutral and non-doctrinaire. But in order to understand the character of places, and the behaviour of people in relation to their environments, we need to probe the motivations, values and emotions of the people involved. Maye draws attention to the fact that the decisions we make about what and how to teach are influenced by our own values and attitudes, for instance towards planning issues, environmental conservation and landscape quality.

Values education in geography is more than the development of an appreciation of the part played by the values and attitudes of people or groups in geographical situations, as the National Criteria emphasize in paragraph 3.7. It provides us with opportunities to assist students to develop their own self-concepts, emotions, values, decision and action skills in a geographical context. Maye suggests that when planning and implementing strategies for values teaching teachers should give careful consideration to the following points:

1 The teacher's own values will influence the topics and stimulus materials chosen and the way in which teaching strategies are implemented.

2 The teacher therefore needs to clarify his/her own values in relation to the topics chosen for study, and be clear in the purpose underlying the approach he/she chooses to follow. With very little change in emphasis and technique, a values analysis strategy could become (intentionally or unintentionally) a values inculcation strategy.

3 An atmosphere of mutual trust and respect in the classroom is necessary for values teaching to be successfully undertaken. Teacher sensitivity is essential.

4 Skilful questioning based on a clear sense of purpose is essential to promoting investigative skills in students.

5 Students should not be pressured into answering or participating in activities about which they are self-conscious. Permit them not to answer or participate if they so choose.

6 Students' responses will be inhibited by teacher moralising, criticism, evaluation of student values, or overt display of the teacher's values.

7 Evaluation of students' learning can be based on their ability to *apply skills* related to valuing in practical activities and situations, rather than on values themselves.

(Maye, 1984, p. 42)

ACTIVITY 8

The question included in Figure 3 appeared in a recent 14–18 Project O-level examination. Does it fairly test the assessment objectives given in paragraph 3.7 of the National Criteria? Does it draw upon any of the approaches suggested by Maye in the quotation in Activity 7? More importantly, does it reflect the intentions and spirit of the kind of geography which is likely to exist in schools as a result of the National Criteria document?

Figure 3   Question from the University of Cambridge Local Examinations Syndicate's 1984 O-level Geography 14–18 Project, Paper 2202/1, pp. 14–15.

The three cartoons are all about the way inner city areas have been re-developed.

(a) Comment on the likely attitudes of **one** of the people shown or mentioned in the cartoons. [5 marks]

(b) Explain how your studies have helped you to see a meaning in the three cartoons. [10 marks]

(c) The residents of decaying inner city areas could be rehoused in new estates on the outskirts of the city.

   (i) Suggest what factors might influence city planners in choosing a location for such an estate. [5 marks]

   (ii) Discuss the disadvantages of this solution to inner city problems and suggest alternatives. [5 marks]

"*Wave bye bye to Gran!*"

HOME
IS WHERE YOUR HEART IS

"THEY'LL NEVER GET ME UP IN ONE OF THOSE THINGS."

"*Be reasonable, madam—we can't have one pedestrian occupying enough space for six units of off-street parking.*"

Teaching and assessing for positive achievement

A major thrust of the new examination will be towards ensuring that candidates are rewarded for their positive achievements (i.e. for showing what they know, understand and can do). Consequently, the General Criteria (para. 16) require that there should be differentiated assessment in all subjects. We begin this session by looking in detail at what is meant by differentiation. We then discuss what we can reasonably expect different groups of students to know and do, and consider the important problem of how to integrate techniques for differentiation into an examination. Finally, we look at some approaches to setting differentiated questions. First, however, the difference between differentiation and discrimination must be established.

2.1 Discrimination and differentiation

Discrimination is concerned with maximizing the spread of marks, and markers are normally encouraged to use the full mark scale. In such a case an examination may well have discriminated between candidates, but it would not necessarily have achieved differentiation in the sense in which the term is used in the criteria documents. Differentiation is concerned with indicating positively what students know and can do, not merely with rank ordering.

In the GCSE examiners will still be required to discriminate between candidates, but they will be required to do so in a particular way—by *differentiation*. Paragraph 16 of the General Criteria is headed 'Differentiated assessment' and states:

> All examinations must be designed in such a way as to ensure proper discrimination so that candidates across the ability range are given opportunities to demonstrate their knowledge, abilities and achievements: that is, to show what they know, understand and can do.

In other words, the need for discrimination is still there, but what is now also needed is that the experience of assessment should be a positive one for all candidates at all levels and that they should be encouraged to demonstrate what 'they know, understand and can do'.

This is a radical departure from current practice where it could be argued that many candidates achieve their marks by relative failure at tasks and where, as a result, they may complete successfully only a small part of the paper. The result is that the examination is often a very unrewarding experience for many candidates. This fact was noted by the Cockcroft Report on mathematics, which said:

> We cannot believe that it can be in any way educationally desirable that a pupil of average ability should, for the purpose of obtaining a school-leaving certificate, be required to attempt an examination paper on which he is able to obtain only about one-third of the possible marks. Such a requirement, far from developing confidence, can only lead to feelings of inadequacy and failure.
> (Committee of Inquiry into the Teaching of Mathematics in Schools, 1982, para. 444)

ACTIVITY 9

Look at a recent GCE O-level or CSE paper in geography. Consider the
O-level paper from the point of view of a candidate likely to obtain
Grade D or E *or* the CSE paper from the point of view of a candidate
likely to obtain Grade 4 or 5. How many questions in the paper could
such a candidate answer successfully? How much of the material,
layout, etc. is inappropriate for such a candidate? Where is the
candidate encouraged and enabled to show what knowledge and
abilities he or she possesses?

On the basis of your answers to these questions, you should be able to begin
to determine what qualities are necessary in a paper designed to differentiate
in the GCSE. You may feel that current papers do not differentiate—indeed,
there is no requirement that they should. This means that assessors—be they
examiners or teachers—face a new challenge in the GCSE, the challenge of
devising forms of assessment that will encourage *all* candidates to
demonstrate what they know, understand and can do.

2.2 *Strategies for differentiation*

Neither the General Criteria nor the National Criteria for geography make
specific requirements that any particular method of achieving differentiation
has to be employed or that only one method of differentiation may be used in
a given examination.

   However, from the current thinking of examiners it has been possible to
identify a number of different strategies for achieving differentiation that are
being considered for use in GCSE examinations so that the fundamental aim
of giving all candidates the opportunity to show what 'they know, understand
and can do' is achieved. The Examining Groups and the Secondary
Examinations Council will be monitoring these different strategies once they
are in operation and will ultimately reach conclusions on their relative
effectiveness. Four main strategies have been identified so far and each is
described briefly below.

Differentiation by outcome

In this strategy differentiation is achieved by giving candidates across the
ability range common or 'neutral' tasks and by identifying different positive
levels of achievement in their responses. For example, in the National
Criteria for English the point is made that a stimulus for writing such as a
personal experience, a picture or an argument can lead to appropriate
writing at all levels of ability within the subject. This technique of a neutral
stimulus—neutral, that is, with respect to difficulty—is one commonly
advocated within the arts and humanities. In geography many enquiry
activities are neutral with respect to difficulty, but students may pursue
them to varying depths. *Mark schemes clearly indicating the expected positive
qualities to be revealed by candidates of differing abilities are essential if this
form of differentiation is to succeed.*

Stepped questions and stepped papers

With stepped questions, the parts of each question are put in ascending order of difficulty, with each part carrying a separate mark. The intention is that the less able candidates will succeed with the early parts of each stepped question and the more able also with later parts. There are several advantages in setting such questions. They offer an attractive format for assessing a set of separate objectives within a single context and they can be used to guide the candidate through a complex topic, thus contributing to the feeling that a worthwhile piece of work has been completed.

With stepped papers, the paper itself is stepped, with the questions arranged in ascending order of assumed difficulty. Candidates may attempt as many questions as they wish, but again the idea is that the abler candidates will make faster progress and succeed in more of the increasingly difficult questions.

However, there are problems with both stepped questions and stepped papers. In particular:

1 Will all examiners and all candidates agree on the hierarchy of difficulty in the paper?

2 Will the fact that by definition part (possibly a large part) of the paper is beyond the less able candidate mean that the examination will not prove a positive experience for many candidates?

Differentiated papers

In this strategy differentiation is achieved by requiring candidates of different abilities to take different papers—in some instances with a common element. In mathematics, for example, normally no papers common to all candidates may be set and at least three 'levels of assessment' must be provided, the lower levels being firmly constrained in their syllabus content.

An important issue which arises in the context of differentiated papers is that of limiting grades. This may be done at either end of the scale: at one end, candidates who sit certain papers may obtain only Grades D, E, F or G; at the other, only A, B, C or D. These schemes place a major responsibility upon the teacher to advise on entry at the appropriate level. This responsibility is sharpened in the case where only Grades A to D are available because there is a risk of a weaker candidate being ungraded (rather than receiving a Grade E). Indeed, on current evidence it would appear that some candidates who deserve to be graded will fail to be, through no fault of their own—something that offends against natural justice. More generally, the curricular and organizational implications of such limited-grade schemes are substantial, especially in mixed-ability classes or in subjects with small entries where there may be only one class. If all candidates follow essentially the same course, it may be unfair if they are limited to one set of papers with a pre-selected range of objectives and content. Moreover, the hierarchy of difficulty of the papers as determined by the examiners may not be universally valid: candidates following different kinds of course under different kinds of organization may perceive the papers differently.

Paragraphs 38–40 of *General Certificate of Secondary Education: a general introduction* (DES/Welsh Office, 1985) deal with the issue of limited-grade papers and draw attention to the need for some overlap in the ranges of grades available at the different levels of assessment.

Papers with differentiated sections

Here the more difficult section or sections are to be attempted only by the abler candidates. Many of the issues that apply to stepping and to differentiated papers also apply to this strategy.

The discussion of strategies for differentiation has been largely in terms of examination papers because most of the thinking about differentiation has concentrated upon them. But the same approaches can be readily translated into the context of coursework. The choice is between (a) presenting the same task to all and differentiating by outcome; (b) structuring and stepping the task so that more able candidates move through to more demanding sub-tasks while the less able still face worthwhile and challenging activities; and (c) assigning different tasks to different groups of candidates according to their ability. For example, a piece of coursework based on the use of an Ordnance Survey map could incorporate a variety of activities targeted at students of differing abilities.

2.3 Levels of achievement in geography

The educational case for positive achievement presented in Section 2.1 of this guide is a convincing one and is an obvious approach to examining. It is an approach which underlies many forms of testing in the world beyond school where graded tests such as those used in gymnastics involve setting realistic targets according to an individual's potential and demand a high degree of mastery from the examinee. Unfortunately, the present approach to public examinations has retained some of the traditions of the old school certificate which, at a time when examinations were mainly a device for identifying those with potential for further study, was concerned with sorting sheep from goats rather than with rewarding achievement.

The National Criteria for geography include a preliminary statement (para. 7, Table 1) on grade descriptions which indicates the achievements likely to be shown by candidates awarded Grades F and C on the GCSE seven-point scale. You will notice that these grade descriptions are expressed in positive terms, that is, the Grade F is described in terms of what the candidate is likely to be able to do.

ACTIVITY 10

Table 3 is an extract from a grade-related criteria statement by the Scottish Examination Board (SEB). Grade-related criteria (GRC) are the criteria over which a candidate will have to demonstrate a given degree of mastery to achieve a particular grade. The SEB has done a great deal of piloting of GRC within the context of their new single system of examining. The table shows the achievements expected of a candidate in geographical knowledge and understanding at three points on a seven-point scale, where one is the highest grade. It is not wise to try to equate the grades too closely with GCSE grades, but you could use Table 3 opposite, paragraph 7, Table 1, in the National Criteria for geography as well as your knowledge of your own students to consider the following questions, which are all concerned with the differences between students.

Table 3 Knowledge and understanding.

	Grade 6	Grade 5	Grade 2
Summary GRC	The pupil has demonstrated, at a simple level, knowledge and understanding of the vocabulary, ideas and concepts developed during the geography course.	The pupil has demonstrated, at a simple level, knowledge and understanding of the vocabulary, ideas and concepts developed during the geography course, can offer simple explanations and can recognize further examples.	The pupil has demonstrated a consistently thorough knowledge and understanding of the vocabulary, ideas and concepts developed during the geography course and has applied them to both familiar and unfamiliar situations to develop hypotheses and generalizations.
Extended GRC	The pupil can demonstrate at a simple level: 1 A knowledge of basic geographical terms used in the course. 2 An understanding of: (a) basic geographical terms by using them in a correct context; (b) key ideas developed during the course. 3 An awareness and understanding of key concepts by showing an ability to recognize them in familiar situations.	In addition, the pupil can demonstrate: 1 An understanding of key ideas and be able to offer a simple explanation of them. 2 An awareness and understanding of key concepts by showing an ability to recognize them in an unfamiliar situation.	In addition, the pupil can demonstrate: 1 An ability to understand and use with consistent accuracy a wide range of geographical terminology. 2 An ability to develop the key ideas and apply them to a wide variety of situations. 3 An awareness of the key concepts, ability to recognize them in new situations and to apply them in hypothetical situations.
Examples of extended GRC	1 Describe a landscape using terms such as hill, mountain, valley, river, farm and village. 2 (a) As above. (b) Key idea—'Manufacturing industry is concentrated in certain parts of the world'—know that Western Europe and Japan have more manufacturing industry than Africa or South America. 3 Recognize that urban renewal in their own city/town is an example of change (Key concept: change).	1 Be able to suggest why there is a concentration of manufacturing industry in the West Midlands in terms of central position and total resources. 2 Given the locational factors for a hydro-electric scheme in the Highlands of Scotland suggest where a hydro-electric scheme might be found in Norway (Key concept: location).	2 From a study of the distribution of manufacturing industry in Western Europe reach generalizations regarding the location of such industries. 3 From a study of an urban renewal project in an area unfamiliar to them be able to recognize the key concept of change, and be able to suggest similar areas where the concept can be applied.

Source: Scottish Examination Board/Joint Working Party in Geography, *Experimental Guidelines for Foundation Level Geography,* Table 5.9, pp. 15–15a.

1 What different kinds of ability between more and less able students are implied by the two tables?

2 Is there a continuum of achievement in geography across the ability range or are there any distinct 'changes of gear', for instance at O-level Grade C or CSE Grade 1? If so, what characterizes this change?

3 Do certain groups of students—boys rather than girls, for example—perform more or less well in some aspects of geography than in others? If so, in what ways?

4 Given the gaps in ability implied by the two tables and the desirability of positive achievement, can all students follow the same kind of geography programme with profit?

These questions in Activity 10 challenge some fundamental principles on which the organization of the school curriculum and the examination system has until now been based, but it is important to consider whether we should continue to expect our students to take examinations that can be likened to a steeplechase in which only a small proportion of the competitors successfully complete the course and many fall at the earliest and lowest hurdles.

2.4 Matching assessment tasks to candidates' abilities

Figure 4 is typical of the photographs which appear in many O-level and CSE examination papers that include data stimulus/response questions. It shows the site of a suburban superstore under construction and it lends itself to teaching and assessing a number of key ideas which might be studied in a geography course. The ones listed below can be found in the GYSL (Avery Hill) 14–16 Geography Project's GCE/CSE syllabus offered jointly by the Southern Universities' Joint Board and the Welsh Joint Education Committee.

> Increased car ownership and changing shopping habits are affecting the character and location of shopping centres.
>
> Movement to work, services, shopping and leisure varies from one individual to another. In some neighbourhoods the range of provision necessitates less movement than in others.
>
> There is often outward movement of city population as the demand for better housing and space standards is met by new house construction at the periphery.
>
> It is important that in planning urban areas due thought be given to the needs of all members of the community.
>
> Local and national decentralization may be caused by 'push' and 'pull' factors.

This photograph could be used both as a teaching aid and as a data item in examination questions designed to test geographical ideas related to urban and economic geography and the skills of photograph interpretation specified in the National Criteria (para. 3.6(ii)). But what could we expect students of different abilities to do with it in a learning or examination situation? More precisely, what assessment tasks could we set using the photograph at which

Figure 4   The site of a new superstore in north Leeds.

students of different abilities could be expected to achieve a high degree of mastery (say 80 per cent)?

ACTIVITY 11

Using the photograph in Figure 4 as a data source or stimulus, try to identify a variety of assessment tasks that could be derived from the key ideas listed and that would be appropriate to the abilities of:

1 A Grade A O-level candidate (GCSE A Grade).

2 A Grade C O-level/CSE Grade 1 candidate (GCSE C Grade).

3 A CSE Grade 4 candidate (GCSE F Grade).

For example a GCSE F Grade task might be:

Give one reason why the superstore has been built at this major road junction;

while an A Grade task might be:

Using information from the photograph to illustrate your answer, explain how increasing car ownership is influencing the location of retailing in urban areas.

You could continue this activity using other data items of your own.

2.5 *Relating grades to performance criteria*

In tackling Activity 11 you used as your starting point your own knowledge of what students who achieve certain grades can do. You then devised tasks that would allow them to show their capabilities. Another approach would be to start by asking what candidates ought to be able to do to be awarded certain grades. Standards in GCSE geography are likely to be determined as much by the second as the first approach.

By relating grades to absolute standards expressed as specific criteria there is an opportunity, provided that the criteria are realistic, for a much higher percentage of candidates to achieve worthwhile grades than under the present norm-referenced system. In order to establish the performance criteria which can be related to each grade, it is necessary to identify a small number of domains or key aspects of the subject within which various specific abilities can be listed. You may have already read the report of the Working Party for the Development of Grade Criteria for geography (Secondary Examinations Council, 1985), which proposes the following five domains: specific geographical knowledge; geographical understanding; map and graphic skills; application of geography to economic, environmental, political and social issues; and geographical enquiry. Two of the domain definitions are given below:

C *Map and graphic skills*
This domain refers to the ability to extract and use geographical information from maps, graphs, diagrams and pictorial material and to communicate information using maps, graphs, diagrams and pictorial material.

In particular it involves the ability to:
(a) extract geographical information from a variety of sources;
(b) interpret the information;
(c) communicate geographical information using appropriate maps, graphs, diagrams and pictorial material.

D *Application of geography to economic, environmental, political and social issues*
This domain refers to the ability to apply geographical ideas and skills to an interpretation of the issues associated with social and economic patterns, the use of resources and the management of the environment.

In particular it involves the ability to:
(a) identify issues arising from the relationship between human activity and environments;
(b) appreciate that different groups of people perceive these issues in different ways according to their own values and experience;
(c) recognise that conflicting demands on resources and space may give rise to problems and that these problems and their possible solutions may be influenced by the values and perceptions of decision makers;
(d) propose, analyse and make judgements about different ways of resolving an issue.

(Secondary Examinations Council, 1985, pp. 8–9)

Once finalized, these domain definitions could form the basis for specifying precise criteria for selected GCSE grades in geography under each domain heading. It would then be possible to devise differentiated assessment tasks for each domain and grade. For example, to obtain a Grade F a candidate might be required, within the map and graphic skills domain, to extract specific items of information from an Ordnance Survey map, such as the distance between two points or the height of a hill. To obtain a Grade A, on the other hand, a candidate could be asked to describe aspects of the physical and human landscape of the map area, which requires a much more selective and subtle extraction, interpretation and synthesis of information.

ACTIVITY 12

In the example we have just cited the progression of difficulty is from a basic facility with map conventions to an ability to analyse and synthesize information extracted from maps.

Consider ways in which progressions of difficulty might be built into the performance criteria for one of the four other domains.

Try to develop examples of assessment tasks for the key GCSE grades (A, C, F) for some of the abilities listed in the domain definitions given earlier.

Domains of geography, each having specific criteria-related grades, could be very helpful to both teachers and Examining Groups. Teachers would have a very clear indication of what to teach and what would be expected of students of different abilities, and Examining Groups would have clear guidance on the required levels of difficulty at which to pitch examination papers or questions.

However, there are problems associated with criteria-based teaching and assessing. For example, relatively simple tasks that may form the basis for assessing lower ability students, such as the ability to extract data from a climate graph, may also be regarded as fundamental for all students. Should higher ability students have to demonstrate their ability at low-order as well as high-order tasks or can the low-order tasks be subsumed within higher-order ones?

ACTIVITY 13

Given that Examining Groups will be required to assess domain abilities separately, and that teachers, employers and students will have access to the criteria for each grade, what are the advantages and disadvantages of an examining system based on well-publicized grade criteria?

Among the advantages you will probably have identified are:

1 Clearer guidelines for mixed-ability teaching.

2 More predictable examination questions in terms of the general abilities to be tested.

3 A sound basis on which to make judgements about entry to any differentiated components of the examination.

2.6 Achieving differentiation in geography

Some of the early proposals for GCSE geography syllabuses include in their schemes of assessment common papers that have inclines of difficulty within and between questions. As we pointed out earlier, if all candidates have to attempt easier and harder questions this is not differentiation in the true sense. However, a case for common papers in geography can be based on the nature of the subject and not just on the wish to avoid the need to select candidates for differentiated papers. Common papers could be used to test achievement in certain basic skills, such as the ability to recall a core of factual information about places or regions specified in the syllabus, the ability to extract information from an Ordnance Survey map for a specific purpose or the ability to use a simple shopping survey sheet in the field. However, such papers (if they were designed to provide realistic targets for the majority) would provide few opportunities for the more able candidates to show what they know and can do.

ACTIVITY 14

Which of the following topics for study could most easily include common tasks and which require tasks to be matched to student ability?

1 Farming systems

2 Urban climate

3 Mental maps

4 Industrial location

5 Place preference

6 Map work

What common tasks do you include in your current courses to provide all students with the opportunity to produce a worthwhile response. Is it appropriate to assess student performance on these tasks? If so, how?

2.7 Differentiated schemes of assessment

Schemes of assessment that include differentiated components will need to meet the following criteria:

1 They should work to the advantage of students by permitting them to achieve their maximum potential.

2 They should help teachers and students to make informed decisions about entry to the differentiated components.

3 They should be so structured that all students can pursue a similarly stimulating and useful programme of learning.

Several geography examinations that use differentiated schemes of assessment are already available. We look at one of them here in order to demonstrate how different forms of differentiation can be employed to achieve both assessment and curricular goals.

The Midland Examining Group's Joint GCE O-level/CSE Examination based on the work of the Schools Council Geography 14–18 (Bristol) Project includes a coursework component made up of three units of work devised by the teacher. These units are introduced at intervals during a two-year teaching programme and occupy about two weeks of normal teaching and homework time. Coursework such as this offers a number of advantages within a differentiated scheme. Tasks can be designed to have an incline of difficulty within and between units and alternative paths through a unit can be provided for different students. They can be given immediate feedback on their progress and the teacher has a basis for counselling the student on entry to other parts of the assessment programme. Another valuable feature of this kind of coursework assessment is the opportunity it offers to assess abilities not easily tested in traditional examinations.

A geographical enquiry or investigation, assessed initially by the teacher, is likely to feature in most GCSE geography examinations. The Midland Examining Group examination has two assessment routes. The more demanding route enables students to undertake an individual study on a topic of their own choice. They are guided at crucial stages by the teacher and may seek advice but are expected to show initiative and imagination. For other students, the investigation is structured and led by the teacher. Here then, differentiation is achieved by setting tasks which differ in terms of the degree of teacher support. Students who set out on very similar enquiries, such as a survey of the provision of medical facilities in a town, and who take different approaches to the task can still be differentiated by outcome rather than by the extent to which they have met the requirements of a common, closely defined task.

Paragraph 6.2.2 of the National Criteria emphasizes the wealth of data available in geography which could be used as question stimuli. Externally set examinations are likely to make considerable use of data response questions. However, while some candidates can easily grasp the geographical implications and complexities of, say, a map showing the distribution of supermarkets and independent grocers, and can write at some length about it, others need carefully structured questions requiring short answers to enable them to demonstrate what they know and can do. To achieve differentiation between these two admittedly broad groups, the Midland Examining Group's examination includes alternative papers based upon common data items. In one paper the questions are relatively open-ended; in the other they are more closely structured. The choice between these two papers can be delayed until late in the course because they are based on a common syllabus.

This scheme of examination exemplifies how a variety of approaches to differentiation can be matched to the different activities which are likely to form part of any geography course.

ACTIVITY 15

If you have time, it would be useful to look at any available schemes of differentiated assessment.

Discuss the contribution these schemes make to developing acceptable approaches to differentiated assessment by considering how they:

1 Safeguard the interest of students.

2 Help effective choice of assessment routes.

3 Recognize different kinds as well as levels of ability.

4 Conform to the General and National Criteria.

As we have already mentioned, one approach to examining is to use the same data on alternative papers but to set different tasks relating to that data. The following two activities explore this approach.

ACTIVITY 16

This activity is derived from papers in the East Anglian Examinations Board/University of Cambridge Local Examinations Syndicate 16+ Examination for June 1983. Below are two sets of questions based on the information in Figures 5a and 5b.

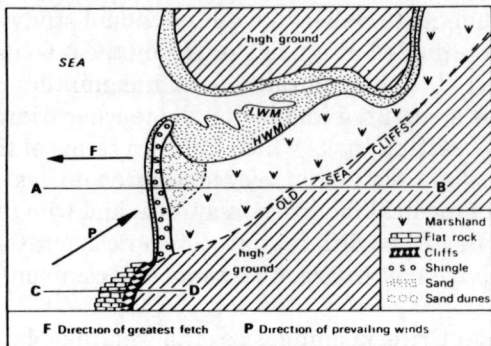

Figure 5a

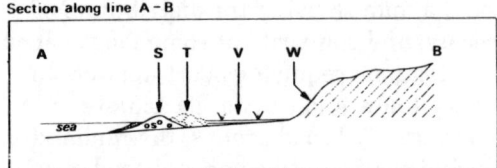

Figure 5b

Question X

(a) (i) What is meant by the 'fetch' of a wave?
(ii) Explain how differences in fetch affect the kinds of waves which arrive at the coast and the work which they do. [6]
(b) With reference to the map and the cross-section, describe the appearance and explain the formation of the features S, T and V on the cross-section along the line A–B. [8]
(c) (i) On your answer paper, draw a sketch section along the line C–D shown on Figure 5a and label the features which it shows.
(ii) Use your diagram to explain the processes by which cliffs were formed here. [10]

Question Y

(a) On your answer paper, name the features on cross-section Figure 5b which are marked by the letters
(i) S; (ii) T; (iii) V; (iv) W. [4]
(b) For feature S on the cross-section (Figure 5b) marked ºsº on the map (Figure 5a),
(i) describe its appearance,
(ii) explain how it may have been formed,
(iii) name an example of this type of feature. [10]
(c) Explain how the marshland shown on the map (Figure 5a) developed. [2]
(d) (i) What is meant by the term *fetch*?
(ii) What conditions give rise to the most powerful waves? [4]
(e) On your answer paper, draw a sketch section along the line C–D shown on the map (Figure 5a) and label the features fully. [4]

1 Do the questions test different abilities or do they test similar abilities in different ways?

2 Which is meant to be the harder question?

3 What do these questions suggest about the perceived differences between CSE Grade 1/O-level Grade C candidates and CSE Grade 2–CSE Grade 5 candidates?

4 Do the questions conform to the National Criteria?

5 Are the data suitable for testing the whole range of abilities?

ACTIVITY 17

Figure 6 is a data item used in the East Midland Regional Examinations Board/University of Cambridge Local Examinations Syndicate Joint GCE O-level/CSE Examination based on the Geography 14–18 Project (June 1985). The question set on this data item is given below and comes from the harder paper.

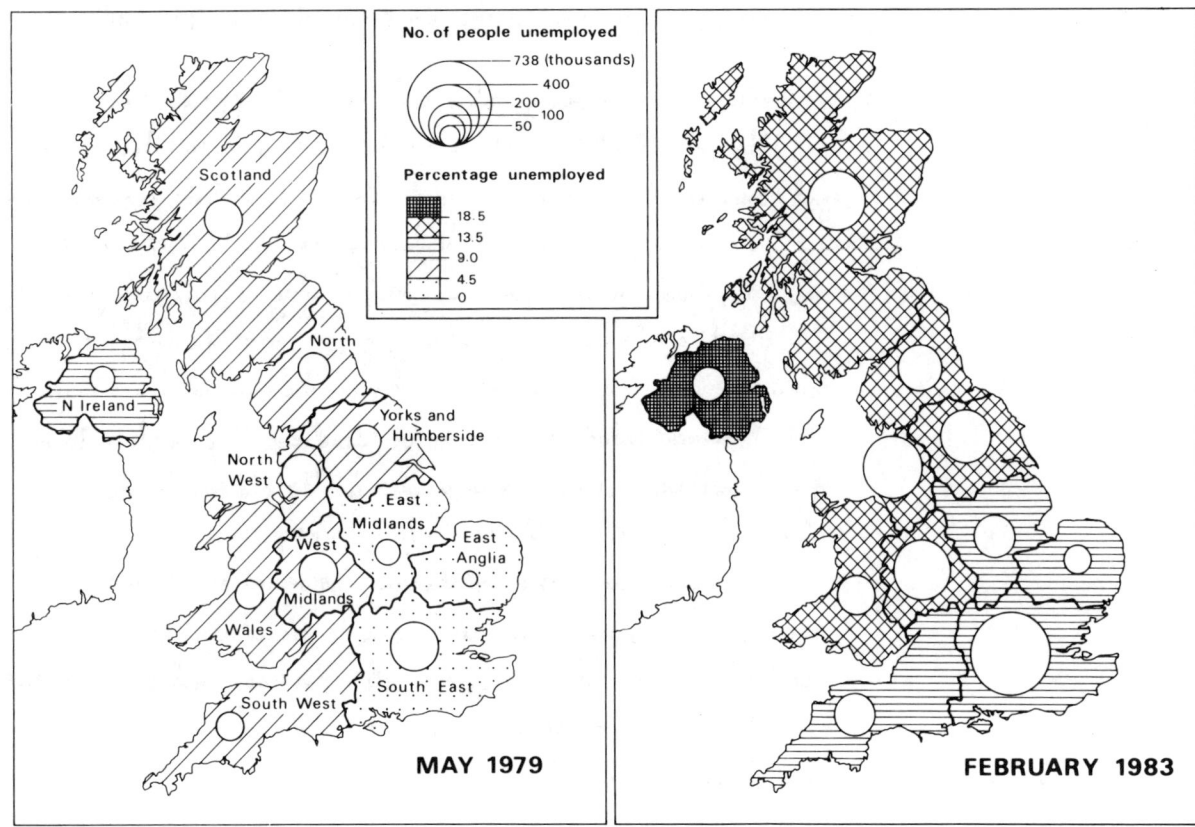

Figure 6

(a) Figure 6 shows the distribution of unemployment in the United Kingdom by the eleven 'standard regions' in 1979 and 1983.
(i) Use the maps to compare changes in unemployment in the South-East region with those in Northern Ireland between 1979 and 1983. [6]
(ii) A line drawn from the Severn to the Humber is said to divide the United Kingdom into two nations. Does evidence on the maps support this view? [6]

(b) A British geographer, Peter Hall, writing about the future geography of the United Kingdom has made the following statements.
(i) 'Tomorrow's industries are not going to be born in yesterday's regions.'
(ii) 'Britain's future, if it has one, is in that broad belt that runs from Oxford and Winchester through the Thames valley and Milton Keynes to Cambridge.'
(iii) 'The aim of government should be to start planning for a massive move of people from old areas and cities to the new.'

Choose one of these statements and suggest why Peter Hall takes this view. Say whether or not you agree with him and suggest arguments against his point of view.   [13]

To what extent does this question permit differentiation through outcome, i.e. where are there opportunities to credit different kinds of response rather than expected or 'correct' ones? Does the question draw upon candidates' awareness of the role of values and attitudes, including their own, in geographical contexts; if so, is the question a fair one to ask?

Figure 7 is one student's response to part (b) of the question. How would you grade it in relation to the demands of the question?

> Peter Hall probably takes this view for several reasons:
>
> (i) Modern industries need to be situated in areas that have good communications, especially roads for door to door delivery, and that have modern purpose built buildings out of the centre of towns.
>
> (ii) These modern industries need a highly skilled workforce, which is not available in 'yesterdays regions' where the workforce was concerned with heavy industries, whereas the new ones are light.
>
> (iii) The new industries have to be developed by people with a fresh outlook, whereas many people in the old areas are rather conservative in the approach to change.
>
> I agree with this statement, however as an argument against it I would say that there is large workforce available in the older regions, with readily available facilities, and that the workforce would be willing to train for the the chance of work.

Figure 7 A student's response to part (b).

You might like to finish by writing a compatible question for candidates likely to achieve a CSE Grade 2–5.

Coursework assessment

In this session you are invited to consider:

1 The reasons why all GCSE geography examinations must include school-based assessment.

2 The purposes served by the internally assessed component of the new examination.

3 The ways in which differentiated assessment can be achieved through coursework.

4 How you might capitalize on the new opportunities offered by school-based assessment.

3.1 The argument for school-based assessment

The National Criteria for geography state that 'all Mode 1 schemes of assessment must include a board-based and a school-based component' and that 'the latter should account for at least 20 per cent of the marks' (para. 6.1). Despite the understandable reservations felt by some teachers and others about work that is internally assessed during a course of study, there is a substantial body of evidence which suggests that coursework can not only provide reliable and valid forms of assessment but can also contribute to the improvement of the curriculum. For example, Torrance (1982) in a report on the problems and possibilities associated with Mode 3 examining concluded that it can improve teachers' abilities to set objectives and assess performance and can enhance the quality of teaching and learning.

ACTIVITY 18

1 Paragraph 6.1 of the National Criteria states that 'strategies for assessment should be capable of measuring the whole range of assessment objectives'. In your opinion (or that of your group) which of the assessment objectives set out in Section 3 of the National Criteria can best be assessed by means of a school-based component? Are there any which you would be prepared to say could *only* be assessed internally?

2 Are there any aspects of the geography course or courses that you currently teach which are assessed by coursework? Are there any parts which are not already assessed in this way but would lend themselves to such an approach?

3 Can coursework be used with advantage to extend the range of assessment techniques available for use with all or only some students?

4 Do the advantages outweigh the disadvantages of school-based assessment in geography for:
  (a) the students;
  (b) the teacher;
  (c) the Examination Boards?

3.2 The purposes served by internally assessed components

The General Criteria (para. 28) make it clear that within board-based schemes of examining internally assessed components may serve one or more of the following purposes:

(a) to assess objectives which cannot be assessed externally;
(b) to assess objectives different from those for a written component;
(c) to provide a complementary assessment of the same objectives as a written component;
(d) to assess objectives for which there is only ephemeral evidence. [In geography, oral work, practical work and fieldwork might fall into this category.]

You may already have had some experience of coursework assessment in the form of fieldwork projects or files in a CSE or A-level examination. Clearly, fieldwork fits very well into the categories of work listed above. However, coursework assessment could be applied more widely than just to field-based activities. The assessment of coursework is one part of any teacher's day-to-day responsibilities for evaluating a geography course (it usually takes the form of homework marking). The work that a student undertakes during a course needs to be assessed in order to evaluate the effectiveness of the course, to monitor student progress and to provide feedback. Coursework assessment, therefore, may readily be seen as a means of assessing the skills objectives in paragraph 3.6 of the National Criteria, but it could be applied to other assessment objectives, especially in schemes of assessment which allocate more than 20 per cent of available marks to school-based assessment.

ACTIVITY 19

Look closely at the two examples of geography coursework opposite.

1 Do they conform to the aims and assessment objectives set out in Sections 2 and 3 of the National Criteria for geography?

2 Decide whether or not it is possible to justify their inclusion in GCSE courses on the basis of paragraph 28 of the General Criteria, quoted above.

It should be stressed at this point that these examples are not being offered as models for future GCSE coursework. They are simply examples of what has been submitted as GCE O-level and/or CSE coursework in recent years. It may well be that the Examining Groups and their subject committees will propose forms of GCSE school-based assessment which are markedly different from the examples provided here. While you are reading them, jot down any thoughts which you have about their suitability for GCSE candidates across the full range of ability—a matter you will be asked to discuss in Activity 20.

Example 1   A study of natural hazards

The students who undertook this assignment were at the end of their fourth year in two neighbouring schools, one a grammar school and the other a secondary modern. Despite selection at the age of eleven, the secondary modern regularly has some students who are capable of obtaining Grades A and B in GCE O-level geography. The assignment came at the end of a unit of work on physical geography and in this piece of coursework the students were asked to study and write about the impact of a natural hazard. The teacher had assembled a variety of resources such as articles from *The Geographical Magazine* and the *National Geographic,* extracts from newspapers, recordings from radio and television broadcasts, filmstrips, slide-sets and works of literature. Allowing the students to choose one hazard from a list of three helped to ease the problem of access to resources during the preliminary research phase of the work. Most of the students' research was undertaken during lesson time over a two-week period during which they were not allowed to remove any of the resources from the classroom. Most of the writing-up was completed for homework. Given below are the instructions which the teachers provided. Notice how they set some precise limits to the length of each task.

Imagine that each of the following disasters has taken place:

1 An earthquake in southern Italy.

2 A volcanic eruption near an Icelandic fishing village.

3 A severe hurricane which has struck an island in the Caribbean.

Task 1

Imagine that you are a newspaper reporter in one of these places when the disaster occurred. You are the first to get your news story back to London. Write your report, making it as factual and dramatic as possible. It must be no longer than 500 words because of the difficulty of getting any messages out of the area.

Task 2

You are now the field director of an international relief agency. As soon as the news came through that the disaster had occurred you were sent out to the area to assess the situation and report back to headquarters on the type of aid required immediately and within the following two weeks. Try to suggest in what order your requests should be met and to give some idea as to how the aid should be routed to reach you. This report should be no longer than one side of A4 paper.

Task 3

The national government of the country in which the disaster occurred has appointed you as minister in charge of the rehabilitation and reconstruction of the area. Write a report on what you see as the disaster area's longer-term needs once the immediate problems have been overcome. Two sides of A4 paper should be adequate for your purpose.

Example 2   A school litter survey

This piece of coursework was attempted by all of the fourth-year students taking geography at a suburban comprehensive school where they are taught in mixed-ability groups and follow a common syllabus. The idea was to give all the students, irrespective of their ability, the experience of participating in a geographical enquiry which had been structured for them by their teachers. In so doing, it was hoped that they would acquire various skills and insights into the enquiry process, which would enable them to go on to tackle an individual study of their own choice (subject of course to the guidance of a teacher and approval by an Examination Board moderator). The choice of a litter survey on the school campus had the advantage of getting students out of the classroom to do fieldwork at no cost and with minimum inconvenience. It also came at a time when the school, the residents' association and the local council were conducting a cleanliness campaign. The fieldwork was undertaken during a double lesson, the students working in groups of three or four, each group being responsible for collecting data within a radius of 1.5 metres of about five of the sites marked on Figure 8. At the end of the lesson the students entered up their data on a master record sheet like the one shown in Figure 9. This was then photocopied for use during the next double lesson when the students began work on the tasks given below. They were allowed no more lesson time but they were given three weeks of homework time to complete their work before handing it in to be marked.

Figure 8   Litter survey: a map of the school campus.

Now that all of the data have been collected and assembled together on the master record sheet we need to present this information in a more useful form. To do this we are going to use two techniques:
1 A bar graph.
2 A distribution map.

1 *A bar graph to show the main litter types.*
Add up the figures under each of the headings: PAPER; GLASS; METAL; PLASTIC; DOG EXCRETA; OTHER. The total figures you obtain at the base of each column show how frequently the different types of litter occur.
(a) *Draw* a bar graph to show this information using the graph-paper provided.
(b) In a paragraph *describe* what your graph shows.
(c) Suggest possible sources of the different types of litter shown on your graph. Make sure that you *explain* why you have chosen the sources you have.

2 *A distribution map of total litter*
To construct your map:
(a) Add up the figures in each row of the master record sheet—this will give you the total litter count for each site that has been surveyed.
(b) Look at the range of values in the 'TOTAL LITTER' column and divide them up into: VERY DIRTY; DIRTY; AVERAGE; CLEAN; and VERY CLEAN.
(c) Choose an appropriate colour code for the five different levels of pollution and place a correctly coloured 'spot' for each of the data collection sites marked 1–50 on the map [Figure 8]. Remember that the numbers 1–50 on the map correspond to the

numbers 1–50 in the left-hand column of the master record sheet. Complete the key to the map.

(d) *Describe* the distribution of litter shown on your map.

(e) Attempt to *explain* why the distribution of litter is like it is. In order to do this you would probably find it helpful to collect some information about one or more of the following: (i) sources of litter around the school; (ii) the present position of litter bins; (iii) busy areas; (iv) wind traps and dead ends.

3 *Planning for change*

Imagine that you have been put in charge of a project to help keep the school campus cleaner. Bearing in mind the results of the survey and what you know about the behaviour of people around the school:

(a) Mark on your 'Litter distribution map' where you would place five new litter bins so that they would have the most benefit.

(b) Carefully *explain* why you chose the sites that you did.

LOCATION	LITTER TYPE						TOTAL LITTER	CODE
	PAPER	GLASS	METAL	PLASTIC	DOG EXC.	OTHER		
1	9	0	4	10	0	0		
2	2	0	6	11	0	0		
3	2	22	0	6	0	1		
4	0	0	1	0	0	0		
5	4	1	1	4	0	1		
6	0	0	1	0	0	1		
7	0	1	1	10	0	4		
8	8	3	3	4	0	12		
9	7	0	0	15	0	7		
10	12	0	2	5	0	0		
42	2	0	0	2	1	0		
43	1	0	0	0	0	1		
44	0	0	0	0	0	1		
45	0	0	0	1	0	2		
46	3	0	1	12	3	0		
47	4	0	1	11	0	3		
48	2	1	1	4	0	1		
49	3	0	1	4	0	2		
50	3	0	0	2	0	0		
TOTALS FOR LITTER TYPE								

Figure 9 Litter survey: master record sheet.

3.3 *Differentiated assessment through coursework*

As we discussed in Session 2, paragraph 16 of the General Criteria makes it clear that 'All examinations must be designed in such a way as to ensure proper discrimination so that candidates across the ability range are given opportunities to demonstrate their knowledge, abilities and achievements'. It goes on to say that, with regard to coursework, 'differentiation will be achieved by presenting candidates with tasks appropriate to their individual levels of ability'. In other words, whatever procedures are adopted, the main aim should be to set tasks which make it possible for students of all abilities to show positive achievement. The following activity invites you to consider how this might be achieved.

ACTIVITY 20

1 Of the two examples of geography coursework you considered in Activity 19 which do you consider to be better suited for use with GCSE candidates across the full range of ability?

2 How would you suggest that the examples be modified to enable all students whatever their ability, to demonstrate what they 'know, understand and can do'?

3 What forms of coursework do you consider to have the greatest potential for ensuring that 'candidates across the ability range are given opportunities to demonstrate their knowledge, abilities and achievements'? How would you justify your choice?

3.4 *Capitalizing on coursework*

The examples considered so far show that coursework can be much more than just routine homework and fieldwork exercises. On the other hand, however imaginative and innovative coursework assignments are, it is essential that they are consistent with the aims and assessment objectives outlined in the National Criteria for geography. However, the guidelines for school-based assessment in GCSE geography do allow for a variety of approaches to coursework. It is to be hoped, therefore, that geography teachers will respond to this aspect of the new examination in a positive and creative way and see it as a means by which they can innovate and, in so doing, enrich the curriculum for all of their students.

For example, judging from what is said in the National Criteria for geography, it seems likely that new subject content will figure in GCSE syllabuses alongside that with which teachers are already familiar. Thus coursework in humanistic and behavioural geography should offer opportunities for teachers to develop their students' 'sense of place' (para. 2.1.1), especially through 'experiential learning' (para. 4.1.1). Similarly, coursework based on the ideas of welfare and radical geography should enable students to develop their knowledge and understanding of 'the geographical aspects of important social and environmental issues' (para. 4.1.4).

ACTIVITY 21

Given below are some topics which could be investigated through coursework. No attempt has been made to categorize them, but they all seem to be consistent with the aims and assessment objectives for the new examination, as stated in the National Criteria. As you read through them, try to identify those topics which you think:

1 Would lend themselves to an enquiry approach in which a question is examined or a hypothesis is tested.

2 Could best be undertaken using other styles of investigation.

3 Would be suitable for activities involving a whole class.

4 Would be better if they were tackled by individuals or small groups.

Suggested topics

- A study of what should be done with a disused section of an old railway line.

- A comparative study of the mental maps of a city centre held by students from an inner-city and a suburban school or by students of different ages or gender from the same school.

- The analysis of a television programme or film of geographical interest which is relevant to the syllabus.

- An examination of the identity of places based, for example, on descriptions by writers, pictures, photographs and interviews.

- A comparison of the images of places held by students with different cultural backgrounds, for example, the image black, white and other adolescents have of the Caribbean.

- Mapping 'nuisance fields' around, for example, a lorry park, factory, quarry, public refuse tip or football ground, based upon observation and interviews with local residents.

- A study of the geography of the economic recession in Britain, based on, for example, local and regional variations in the distribution of employment and unemployment, opening and closure of factories, offices and shops.

- An investigation into the contrasting attitudes of farmers and other interest groups towards such things as hedgerows, moorlands, and wetlands.

- An analysis of the procedures by which planning decisions are reached, for example, the route for a stretch of motorway.

- 'The good, the bad and the ugly', an alternative to the official guide to a town or a tourist area.

- The study of the landscape of an area as seen through the work of artists, for example, Constable's Suffolk and Lowry's northern England.

- A record of a sensory walk through an area.

- A study of the place knowledge of the residents of an area based upon interviews, for example, with people who have lived there for a long period.

Coursework based on topics such as these would involve students in using evidence provided by photographs, film, television, radio, newspaper, magazines, and works of art and literature. As such, it would complement the primary data which they had collected by means of fieldwork and information obtained from more familiar secondary sources such as census returns, parish registers, reference books and periodicals.

This suggests that the form of the response or the end-product submitted by the students for assessment should be equally varied. Systematic and well-organized fieldwork reports with their statutory maps, graphs and diagrams based on data collected at first hand are one form of written response which geography teachers might reasonably expect from their students as coursework—but not the only one. For example, this sort of response would not necessarily be the most appropriate way of reporting a sensory walk through a place or a townscape appreciation study. Additionally, an extended piece of writing might not be the best way to stimulate and motivate students across the full range of ability either to learn or to demonstrate what they 'know, understand and can do'. This is not to say that writing in geography should be neglected. Indeed, on the basis of the advice given in the Bullock Report (Committee of Inquiry into Reading and the Use of English, 1975) it is to be hoped that students will be given every opportunity through their geography coursework to communicate their thoughts and feelings in writing. Not only would this contribute to the development of their basic literacy but the process of writing itself should enable them to arrive at a better knowledge and understanding of the ideas under consideration. Thus it is to be hoped that in setting coursework in geography teachers will try to devise a variety of interesting writing tasks which will motivate students of all abilities. Students would also benefit from the chance to discuss their ideas with other students and their teachers and to give oral presentations of their work to other members of the class. In assessment terms this would obviously create fresh challenges for geography teachers. However, the problem in this case might be overcome by the use of some form of oral assessment.

Many of the topics for geography coursework suggested above would offer scope for students to communicate the outcomes of their enquiries by means of film, television, tape-slide sequences, posters and wall displays. Visual images and sounds are powerful means of communication in their own right and they seem to be especially appropriate to a subject such as geography. The educational value of project work which involves the production of audio-visual materials has been clearly demonstrated by Lorac and Weiss (1981). They found that project work of this kind in subjects across the curriculum not only helps to develop students' communication skills but their social skills as well. This is because it creates opportunities for students to collaborate with each other, to make collective decisions and to take on responsibilities—which not only develops their interpersonal skills but promotes their personal development in other ways.

The widespread access which geography departments now have to computers and the growing amount of software available points to this as another area with potential for development through coursework. A brief example from current practice illustrates this potential.

Example 3   Using a data retrieval program

As part of a coursework assignment, the fifth-year students at a large commuter-village comprehensive school gather data about employment and unemployment in the local area by means of a questionnaire. They are taught in mixed-ability groups and follow a common syllabus. The survey produces data on the place of residence of the respondents, their age, gender, employment status (full-time or part-time), length of time employed in their present post or unemployed, place of employment, details of their journey to work and the nature of their employment. Originally, these data were collated into a large data booklet and the resulting data processing and analysis proved to be a lengthy and tedious business for students and teachers alike. This and a dramatic increase in the number of completed questionnaires caused staff to look to the computer as a better method of data storage and retrieval. They turned to the 'INFORM' program produced by the county's Computer Education Centre, which was already being used in the school. This has two parts: 'INFILE' and 'INFORM'. The former allows information to be entered and stored on disk; the latter is used to obtain the information in order to complete particular tasks which are part of the assessed coursework. An instruction booklet enables students to access the data from a BBC B computer and monitor housed in the classroom.

The GCSE and the geography teacher's role

In this final session we begin by considering practical issues concerned with the implementation of school-based assessment. We then ask you to turn your attention to wider professional matters such as participation in the moderation of internally assessed work and curriculum development.

4.1 School-based assessment: what and when to assess

It is evident from what has been said so far in this guide and in the National Criteria (para. 6.3.1) that school-based assessment will take many forms. The detailed requirements for school-based assessment will vary from syllabus to syllabus in the GCSE, but it is likely that assessments will range from:

1 Those which allocate the statutory minimum of 20 per cent of the marks to the internal assessment of fieldwork, which could be in the form of several short pieces of work or one large study, to

2 More elaborate schemes in which a higher proportion of the marks (say 40 per cent or more) is allocated to various forms of coursework, including that done in the field.

Schemes in this second category provide an opportunity to introduce assessment into a variety of activities which normally form part of geography courses. For example, a scheme which allocates 50 per cent of the total marks to coursework might include not only fieldwork enquiries or an individual study with a weighting of say 20 per cent, but also two or three further units of work which assess some of the other skills and competences not easily tested in a timed examination. These tasks could be spaced out during the course in the form of continuous periodic assessment. They could be devised in such a way that they contributed to course objectives by evaluating the output of two or three weeks of study.

ACTIVITY 22

1 Which approach to school-based assessment do you consider to be most appropriate to your circumstances:
    (a) schemes in which the minimum of 20 per cent of the total mark is allocated to fieldwork of various kinds, assessed mainly at the end of the course; *or*
    (b) more elaborate schemes in which a greater proportion of the marks is allocated to coursework of various kinds, assessed at intervals during the two years of the course?
How would you justify your choice?

2 Compile a list of actual and possible activities, including fieldwork, which would in your view satisfy the National Criteria with regard to school-based assessment. How possible do they seem to you:

(a) in your school circumstances;

(b) within the GCSE syllabuses which you have seen for the new examination?

3 What additional resources would you require to implement such approaches? Are there any possibilities of collaboration between schools in your area in order to share certain resources and to co-operate in the joint production of others?

4 The General Criteria state that 'the syllabus, and in particular the scheme of assessment, must not make unreasonable demands on human and financial resources' (para. 19(e)(vii)). Would the changes in your teaching and assessment practices implied by the inclusion of a school-based assessment component in the new examination necessarily increase the pressures on you and your colleagues and on your financial resources?

4.2 Putting school-based assessment into practice

In addition to the questions we have discussed so far, there is a further set of issues which need to be borne in mind when you are considering the implementation of school-based assessment. Fortunately, there is an accumulated wealth of experience among the schools and Examination Boards which have pioneered work of this kind. Given below is a summary of some of the important lessons which have emerged from that experience. It is offered as a starting point for discussing the crucial question of how coursework assessment can be put into practice in schools.

A clear sense of purpose

When devising coursework assignments, irrespective of their nature, experience suggests that both students and teachers benefit from being perfectly clear about purpose. From the students' point of view, clarity of purpose helps them to respond appropriately to the tasks which their teachers have devised. On their side, the teachers need to be clear about the objectives the work is intended to assess. Among other things this enables them to draw up a mark scheme and to identify the assessment criteria which they intended to apply when marking and grading students' work. Figure 10 is an extract from a coursework assignment based upon a shopping survey. The work was divided into four stages:

1 Preparation for fieldwork—students worked in small groups to devise a questionnaire, draw their base maps, etc.

2 Fieldwork—students visited the local town centre where they gathered their data.

3 Follow-up work—students presented their fieldwork in the form of maps and graphs.

4 Writing-up of results.

The extract given in Figure 10 refers to the final writing-up stage of the assignment.

Figure 10   An extract from a coursework assignment (shopping survey).

Written assignment

(a)   Present the information you have collected from the three centres in the form of maps and
      graphs.   (25 marks)

(b)   What observations and conclusions can you make from the information you have gathered?
                                                                                (30 marks)

Remember to include copies of your questionnaire conducted at your local shop/shopping precinct
in an appendix at the back of your assignment.

When marking this assignment we shall be taking the following into consideration:

1   The care you have taken in recording and classifying your information.

2   The techniques which you have used in presenting your information.

3   Your ability to analyse and draw conclusions from the information which you have gathered.

4   Your awareness of the problems in collecting the information and of drawing conclusions from it.

5   The neatness of your work and the standard of your English.

Length of response

It is to be hoped that in assessing their students' work teachers will be
looking for evidence of quality in relation to agreed criteria rather than
length. However, when setting work it is often useful to all concerned to
indicate the length of response expected (see, for example, the coursework
assignment on natural hazards discussed in Session 3, Activity 19,
Example 1). From the students' point of view, this can help them to direct
their answers to the question and to concentrate on organizing and
presenting their material to the best possible advantage. So far as teachers
are concerned, it can help to avoid having long, repetitious and unstructured
material to mark.

Structuring coursework

A related problem is the degree to which coursework assignments should be
structured. Structuring the tasks within a piece of coursework can help the
students to organize their efforts and responses. It can also be used in the
assessment process in that various tasks can be related to different
objectives. For example, in the shopping survey referred to above the
teachers were able to allocate marks to the work undertaken by the students
in relation to each stage of the enquiry (i.e. planning and preparation,
fieldwork, follow-up work and writing the report). When a substantial piece
of work is structured in this way it allows teachers to assess progressively
how students have tackled each task and enables them to assess the 'process'
as well as the 'product'. Thus a sustained piece of work which has been
broken down into stages enables teachers to assess objectives and hence to
reward attributes not normally associated with timed examinations. The
grading of tasks within a coursework assignment can also be used as a means
of achieving differentiation.

Skills and techniques

Some coursework involves the use of special skills and techniques, such as
those required to undertake practical activities in the field or to present
findings in the form of graphs and maps. It is worthwhile spending time
beforehand helping students to acquire these skills and techniques so that
they can use them with confidence.

Guidance given to students

Some students will be more eager than others to seek help; and some teachers may be more inclined than their colleagues to give that assistance. Since one of the main advantages of coursework is that it blurs the distinction between learning and assessment, it is difficult to lay down hard and fast rules. For example, it would seem foolish to refuse to give some guidance to students if it would help them to get started on a task, or to avoid irrelevancy; but it would be unfair if some students were given that assistance while others were denied it. Consequently, this is a matter which needs to be discussed among teachers in order to frame guidelines for future practice. Once agreed, it is important that these guidelines be applied consistently and be reviewed from time to time in the light of experience.

Presentation of work

In order to avoid unnecessary doubt and uncertainty on the part of students, experience suggests that they should be given clear and unambiguous instructions on how their coursework should be presented for assessment. These instructions should also tell students how they could improve the quality of their work, for example by the inclusion of maps, graphs, diagrams and photographs relevant to the assignment.

Allocation of time to coursework assignments

Given the fact that some school-based assessment is likely to be a feature of most subjects in the new examination, care must be taken not to make excessive demands on students. This will not only involve devising assignments which make economic use of their time, but will also require careful planning and co-ordination between departments to prevent students from being faced with more than one piece of coursework at once. Careful thought will also have to be given to what guidance students should receive on such matters as how much time to allocate to a piece of coursework, or how long to take over the various stages in an assignment. Using prescribed amounts of lesson time and setting deadlines for the submission of coursework are two ways in which teachers can help to control the amount of time their students devote to any one piece of work.

Handing in coursework

From the point of view of planning their work and co-ordinating their commitments across the curriculum it is important for students to have a clear indication of what they have to hand in, and when, throughout the duration of their course. They should also be notified in advance about the penalties they will incur if work is handed in late without good reason. The Examining Groups' procedures for genuine cases of special difficulty should be adhered to and teachers are advised to become familiar with them as soon as they become available. Judging from current procedures, these should accommodate cases which arise as a result, for example, of periods of absence on account of illness or transfer from one school to another. From an assessment point of view, a proper set of procedures needs to be established within a geography department so that work can be marked and moderated internally (e.g. to ensure comparability of assessment between teachers) before submission for external moderation.

Marking coursework

Experience shows that some re-direction of a teacher's efforts is necessary if time is to be devoted to the assessment of coursework. The rigorous periodic evaluation of coursework demanded by many schemes of assessment (and the feedback that teachers can give their students) should make it possible for teachers to reduce the amount of their routine marking. The emphasis should be on the quality of the marking and the related feedback to the students after an assessment. Experience also suggests that marking with the guidance of agreed criteria and the cross-moderation of samples of work can improve the reliability of school-based assessment. The publication of the grade-related criteria should be of considerable assistance to teachers in this respect. The prompt marking of coursework and the provision of feedback to students while the work is still relatively fresh in their minds are two further lessons from current practice. With regard to student feedback, the aim should be to write qualitative comments that will improve future learning and promote positive achievement. The marking of coursework also gives teachers useful feedback on such vital questions as the suitability of the tasks which they have devised. For further guidance on these matters, see Tolley and Reynolds (1977).

Record keeping

Irrespective of whether coursework is assessed at intervals during a course or towards the end of it, careful consideration needs to be given to the recording of marks or grades awarded. Some schools will already be familiar with record cards and sheets devised for this purpose. Where the assessment of coursework is undertaken throughout a course, the information stored can yield a useful profile of a student's achievements. The data can also reveal evidence on the effectiveness of the different tasks within a piece of coursework, and can be used in making comparisons of performance on different coursework assignments. The footnote to paragraph 38 of the General Criteria indicates that the Department of Education and Science is aware of the need for Examining Groups to make 'use of carefully designed record cards, forms etc.' which 'can assist the teacher in recording assessments, reduce the clerical tasks involved to the essential minimum'. The footnote goes on to say that this would provide records which would 'enable subsequent moderating procedures to be carried out efficiently'.

Some schools have already begun to experiment with the use of computers to help with the storage, processing, retrieval and analysis of coursework marks. Figures 11 and 12 (overleaf) illustrate what one school has achieved. The school originally designed a program (MARKSORT) for use with the Commodore 4032 computer, 4050 disk drive and 4022 matrix printer. The program is used to create a file of student names (with or without labels such as form, option or set names) which can be up-dated by adding the names of new students and removing the names of those who leave. Marks allocated to internally assessed coursework can be stored, weighted (e.g. converted into percentages), combined into sub-totals or all added together. Selected marks can be used to generate grades and/or ranked to give students' positions. The data generated in these ways can be viewed on a monitor and printed off in a variety of forms (Figure 11). In addition, the program can provide a printout of a dispersion graph (Figure 12) showing the mark distribution of all the students in a set or all the marks awarded in the school to a particular coursework assignment. This is useful in comparing the performance of one teaching set against another and in making comparisons between coursework assignments. As schools acquire more powerful computing facilities and as school-based assessment becomes a feature of the new examination for students in most subjects, it would seem sensible for teachers to explore the possibility of using computers to help them in this important and essential part of their work.

Figure 11 A computer print-out of school-based assessment records.

| NAMES OF CANDIDATES | PAPER 3 | | | | | PAPER 4 | | | 5 |
	UNIT I	UNIT II	UNIT III	RAW TOTAL	WTED TOTAL	UNIT IV	UNIT V	WTED TOTAL	IND STUDY
SMITH ERIC	67.9	50	60	*	*	*	*	*	34
EDWARDS MARTIN	49.4	55	56	*	*	*	*	*	50
JAMES PAT	57.7	67.5	73	*	*	*	*	*	67
WATERS JOAN	41	47.5	56	*	*	*	*	*	40
NORTH JAMES	50.6	56.3	52	*	*	*	*	*	49
GARDNER LINDA	53.8	66.3	63	*	*	*	*	*	64
LYONS KEVIN	10.3	16.3	23	*	*	*	*	*	12
ANDERSON TERENCE	51.3	57.5	62	*	*	*	*	*	*
BARKING LARRY	42.3	47.5	67	*	*	*	*	*	55
KENDALL ANNE	55.1	56.3	49	*	*	*	*	*	36
STONEHEAD ROGER	60.3	71.3	68	*	*	*	*	*	20
LINTON PETER	59	60	61	*	*	*	*	*	55
JONES DENISE	79.5	80	82	*	*	*	*	*	91
SCOTT BRIAN	60.3	70	76	*	*	*	*	*	64
ALLEN JAMES	63.5	50	68	*	*	*	*	*	68
JOHNSON SUSAN	53.8	57.5	68	*	*	*	*	*	57
LEGGE DIANA	57	50	15	*	*	*	*	*	54
GUEST BARBARA	28.2	45	47	*	*	*	*	*	42
ROSE JANE	78.2	71.3	77	*	*	*	*	*	73
WALKER THOMAS	62.8	68.8	69	*	*	*	*	*	41
CARTWRIGHT CAROL	50.6	42.5	49	*	*	*	*	*	37
HUNTER CHRISTINE	39.7	68.8	67	*	*	*	*	*	62
LANG KIM	57.7	50	59	*	*	*	*	*	73
MILLER GEORGE	61.5	63.8	49	*	*	*	*	*	59
DANIELS ALAN	55.1	57.5	46	*	*	*	*	*	38
WESTON SUSAN	51.9	50	75	*	*	*	*	*	47
COWAN CHARLES	47.4	50	49	*	*	*	*	*	55
LEACH DAISY	46.2	52.5	46	*	*	*	*	*	44
SYMMONDS DEREK	52.6	51.3	51	*	*	*	*	*	39
PRICE BRENDA	57.7	71.3	57	*	*	*	*	*	57
FEATHER JOHN	46.8	57.5	58	*	*	*	*	*	51

TEACHER:............ DATE:....... ASSESSOR:............ DATE:......

Notes:

1 Paper 3 refers to the coursework component of the examination in which the students have to do three units of work. The marks given for each of the three units are percentages. The raw totals (column 4) will be out of 300; the weighted total will be out of 50.

2 Paper 4 is an alternative to Paper 5 (individual study). All of the students shown on this record sheet took the Paper 5 option. The marks shown are percentages; they will be weighted later to a mark out of 30.

Figure 12 A computerized mark distribution graph for a coursework assignment.

MARK	FREQUENCY	NO.	TOTALS
70		0	0
69	■	1	
68		0	
67		0	65 – 69
66		0	
65		0	1
64	■■	2	
63	■	1	
62	■■	2	60 – 64
61	■■	2	
60	■■	2	9
59	■■	2	
58	■■	2	
57	■■■	3	55 – 59
56	■■	2	
55	■■■■■■■	7	16
54	■■■	3	
53	■■	2	
52	■■■■	4	50 – 54
51	■■■	3	
50	■■■■	4	16
49	■■■	3	
48	■■	2	
47	■■■■	4	45 – 49
46	■■	2	
45	■■■■■	5	16
44	■■■	3	
43	■■■■■	5	
42	■■■■■	5	40 – 44
41	■■■■■■■	7	
40	■■■■■■■■	8	28
39	■■■	3	
38	■	1	
37	■■■	3	35 – 39
36	■■■■■■	6	
35		0	13
34	■■	2	
33	■■■■	4	
32	■■	2	30 – 34
31	■■■	3	
30	■■■■■	5	16
29	■	1	
28	■	1	
27	■■	2	25 – 29
26	■	1	
25	■	1	6
24	■■■■■	5	
23	■■■■■	5	
22	■■	2	20 – 24
21	■■	2	
20		0	14
19		0	
18	■■	2	
17		0	15 – 19
16		0	
15	■	1	3
14		0	
13	■	1	
12	■■	2	10 – 14
11	■	1	
10		0	4
9		0	
8	■	1	
7		0	5 – 9
6		0	
5		0	1
4	■■	2	
3		0	
2		0	0 – 4
1		0	
0		0	2

NO.= 145   MEAN= 40.3   ST. DEV.= 14

ACTIVITY 23

1 Look back at the two examples of coursework which you discussed in Session 3, Activity 19. To what extent do you think they are consistent with the guidelines given above?

2 How would you tackle the problem of assessing the outcome of these two pieces of work from students across a wide range of activity? For example, would you accept a common marking scheme or would you attempt to devise a set of criteria which could be related to GCSE grades?

3 Having read the guidelines given above, which of the problems seem to you to be most urgent in the context of your school? How do you think they could best be tackled?

Having completed this activity, you might go on to consider the following questions:

1 What examples of good practice in relation to school-based assessment are already available in:
    (a) other subject departments in your own school;
    (b) the geography departments in schools in your area?

2 How applicable to your situation are the examples of good practice you have identified?

4.3 *Moderating school-based assessment*

The General Criteria make it perfectly clear that 'the scrutinising, monitoring and moderating responsibilities must be exercised throughout the examining process' (para. 29). Many teachers will already be familiar with the methods identified in paragraph 31 of the General Criteria, which are used by the Examination Boards to moderate school-based assessment. These can be classified under two broad headings:

    (a) moderation by inspection or re-assessment, in which the candidates' work (or samples of their work) is inspected and the original assessments adjusted as necessary to bring them into line with a general standard;

    (b) statistical moderation, in which the original assessments of the work of a group of candidates are compared statistically with other assessments and the original assessments adjusted as necessary to bring them into line with a general standard.

Whichever method or combination of methods used by the Examining Group whose syllabus you choose to adopt, it is evident that geography teachers can expect moderation procedures to be applied at 'all appropriate stages of the examining process' (para. 34). It seems that this will not only include monitoring standards of marking between schools but also the scrutiny of 'any question paper or other assessment component prepared by a centre or group of centres' to ensure that it 'complies with the requirements of the syllabus' and that 'its demands over the full range of grades to be awarded are comparable with those of the Group's other GCSE examinations in the subject' (para. 36). Thus geography teachers can expect to have their work on all aspects of coursework assessment closely monitored, and in the process the level of their accountability must inevitably increase. For example, teachers in a geography department will be accountable not only to each other for their standards of assessment but also to other schools taking the same examination where group moderation meetings are part of the external moderation process. In other situations teachers will be accountable to a moderator appointed by the Examining Group.

ACTIVITY 24

1 With regard to coursework, what procedures can a school or college geography department adopt in order to achieve comparability of assessment between its members of staff?

2 What appears to you to represent the best of current practice with regard to the external moderation of school-based assessment? How would you justify your choice?

3 What benefits might a teacher expect to derive from participating in the external moderation of a school's internally assessed work?

4.4 *Choosing a GCSE syllabus*

One consequence of the new examination system is that there will be fewer geography syllabuses available at 16+. What is more, those syllabuses will all have to conform to the same set of criteria. However, this does not mean that all the syllabuses and related schemes of assessment will be the same; nor does it mean that schools will be unable to choose between them. Indeed, the General Criteria make it perfectly clear that 'schools and colleges are free to register as examination centres with the Examining Group or Groups of their choice and to enter candidates directly for the subjects and syllabuses of their choice' (para. 68(h)). Even within an Examining Group more than one geography syllabus will be available. Hence it is to be hoped that teachers will give careful thought to the range of GCSE geography syllabuses open to them and make informed professional judgements about them before making their final selection. In arriving at that decision you might find it helpful to consider the following:

1 Do you think the detailed aims and assessment objectives of the syllabus are helpful to the teaching of geography at this level? How consistent are they with the wider goals of your school, particularly with regard to the general educational development of all your students?

2 Does the subject content of the syllabus offer scope for you and your colleagues to capitalize on your interests and expertise? Is it likely to interest both girls and boys and to motivate them across the full range of ability, whatever their cultural backgrounds?

3 What are the requirements for school-based assessment? Will they enable your department to develop an appropriate curriculum for all of the students taking geography? Will teachers and students be capable of coping with the time demands of the scheme?

4 Does your department have the necessary resources to teach a course derived from the syllabus? Will it, for example, enable you to make use of existing resources or to collaborate with other schools in the production and use of new ones?

5 What demands will the syllabus place upon you and your colleagues in terms of your teaching methods and relationships with students? In what ways will existing practices have to change?

6 What system is to be used for moderating school-based assessment? Does the system provide advice on such matters as designing courses and coursework assignments as well as moderating standards? Do the procedures specified in the syllabus seem to you to make reasonable demands on teachers' time and efforts?

7 How consistent will the new courses be with those which your department offers at 11–14 and 16–19? If you adopted the syllabus, what changes would you have to make to your pre-14 and post-16 courses?

8 How helpful are the supporting guidelines to the syllabus provided by the Examining Groups?

9 Do the specimen papers which accompany the syllabus encourage teaching for positive achievement? Will they have a beneficial 'backwash effect' on the curriculum? From an assessment point of view do you think they will facilitate the fair grading of candidates across the full range of ability?

10 Is there a consensus among your colleagues about the suitability of the syllabus? If pressed by, for example, a senior colleague, an LEA inspector or a parent, would you feel confident in your ability to justify your syllabus choice?

ACTIVITY 25

Making use of copies of the outline table provided, apply the list of questions given above to the critical appraisal of GCSE syllabuses. A simple grading system may help you to begin your assessment.

Table 4

	Syllabuses		
	(a)	(b)	(c)
1 Aims and objectives			
2 Subject content			
3 School-based assessment			
4 Resource requirements			
5 Styles of teaching and learning			
6 Moderation procedures			
7 Curriculum continuity			
8 Teachers notes for guidance			
9 Backwash effects			
10 Degree of departmental consensus			

4.5 *Developing the geography curriculum*

It is clear from what has been said so far that we think the advent of the GCSE will require most teachers to develop and exercise new professional skills, not just in the classroom but also in assessing and developing the curriculum. Fortunately, through such activities as those connected with the Geographical Association, CSE Mode 3 examinations and the Schools Council projects, geography teachers have shown a willingness to work collaboratively to meet new challenges as they have arisen. They have thereby built up an invaluable store of experience of school-based curriculum development; and there are well-established networks of teachers and others at the local and regional level in most parts of the country. Although geography departments in many schools are capable of developing their own curriculum and assessment procedures to satisfy the demands of the new examination, we think that the advantages of inter-school co-operation on such matters far outweigh the disadvantages. The extract below discusses the benefits of schools working together in consortia to tackle changes of the sort which teachers now face with the introduction of the GCSE.

> In the last fifteen years much curriculum development has been facilitated by co-operative arrangements between schools. Such groups can bring together schools which differ in ethos and structure, but which have in common the intention of implementing curriculum change in geography. The motivation which prompts inter-school co-operation may vary with the teachers involved, but is likely to include some of the following expectations:
>
> (a) mutal reassurance and support in attempting something new and unfamiliar;
> (b) a division of labour in the preparation of resources;
> (c) the exchange of ideas about the objectives of the curriculum innovation and for developing appropriate structures and materials;
> (d) the development of strategies for school-based assessment and for informal comparison of outcomes;
> (e) the exchange of ideas on teaching methods;
> (f) sharing in teaching resources produced by individual members;
> (g) sharing the use of certain resources and equipment (e.g. for fieldwork and for reprographic processes) ...
>
> It is important that all those affected by curriculum change should have the opportunity both to share in the decision making and to participate in consortium meetings. Where these are in school time there may be a tendency for the same people, often heads of department, to attend regularly. This may be administratively more efficient but is often dysfunctional as a means of managing change and encouraging involvement by all members of the department.
> (Stephenson, 1985)

Geography teachers have become accustomed to change, and may find that the new single system of examining rationalizes many of the developments which have already taken place. Some may consider that the introduction of national criteria will act as a constraint; our view is that they will provide teachers and Examining Groups with opportunities to develop more imaginative and relevant styles of teaching and assessment techniques.

References

BOARDMAN, D. (ed.) (1985) *New Directions in Geographical Education,* Lewes, The Falmer Press, New Directions Series.

COMMITTEE OF INQUIRY INTO READING AND THE USE OF ENGLISH (1975) *A Language for Life: report of the Committee of Inquiry appointed by the Secretary of State for Education and Science under the chairmanship of Sir Alan Bullock,* London, HMSO (Bullock Report).

COMMITTEE OF INQUIRY INTO THE TEACHING OF MATHEMATICS IN SCHOOLS (1982) *Mathematics Counts,* London, HMSO (Cockcroft Report).

DEPARTMENT OF EDUCATION AND SCIENCE/WELSH OFFICE (1985) *General Certificate of Secondary Education: a general introduction,* London, HMSO.

DEPARTMENT OF EDUCATION AND SCIENCE (1985) *Education for All: report of the Committee of Inquiry into the Education of Children from Ethnic Minority Groups,* London, HMSO (Swann Report).

LAWS, K. (1984) 'Learning through field work' in FEIN, J., GERBER, R. and WILSON, P. (eds) *The Geography Teacher's Guide to the Classroom,* Melbourne, Macmillan.

LORAC, C. and WEISS, M. (1981) *Communication and Social Skills,* London, Wheaton.

MAYE, B. (1984) 'Developing valuing and decision making skills in the geography classroom' in FEIN, J., GERBER, R. and WILSON, P. (eds) *The Geography Teacher's Guide to the Classroom,* Melbourne, Macmillan.

SECONDARY EXAMINATIONS COUNCIL (1985) *Report of the Working Party for the Development of Grade Criteria for Geography,* London, SEC.

STEPHENSON, B. (1985) 'Working in a consortium', unpublished paper, Exeter University.

TOLLEY, H. and REYNOLDS, J. B. (1977) *Geography 14–18: a handbook for school-based curriculum development,* London, Macmillan Education.

TORRANCE, H. (1982) *Mode III Examining: six case studies,* York, Longman/Schools Council.

WALFORD, R. (ed.) (1985) *Geographical Education for a Multicultural Society,* Sheffield, Geographical Association.

UNIVERSITY OF LONDON SCHOOL EXAMINATIONS BOARD (1985) *Sexism, Discrimination and Gender Biases in GCE Examinations,* London, University of London School Examinations Board.

Further reading

DEPARTMENT OF EDUCATION AND SCIENCE (1979) *Aspects of Secondary Education in England: a survey by HM Inspectors of Schools,* London, HMSO.

HM INSPECTORATE (1978) *The Teaching of Ideas in Geography,* London, HMSO (Matters for Discussion, No. 5).

HUCKLE, J. (1981) 'Geography and values education' in WALFORD, R. (ed.) *Signposts for Geography Teaching,* London, Longman.

HUCKLE, J. (1982) 'Humanistic geography: an introduction' in WIEGAND, P. and ORRELL, K. (eds) *New Leads in Geographical Education,* Sheffield, Geographical Association.

ORRELL, K. and WIEGAND, P. (1984) *Evaluation and Assessment in Geography,* Sheffield, Geographical Association.

SLATER, F. (1982) *Learning through Geography,* London, Heinemann.